THE WATCHMAN ON THE WALL

Isaiah 1.27 & 28 Zion shall be redeemed with judgment, and her converts with righteousness...and the destruction of the transgressors and of the sinners shall be together.

AND THEY THAT FORSAKE THE LORD SHALL BE CONSUMED

LIFTING UP MY VOICE LIKE A TRUMPET TO WARN OF

GOD'S JUDGMENT OF AMERICA

Written by: Elder E.L. Staley

January 12, 1995

How the Devil Tried to Destroy Me

My Testimonies of How God Spared My Life

ISBN: 0-75963-210-3

This book is printed on acid free paper.

1stBooks-rev. 7/17/01

"THE MAKING OF A PROPHET"

Hello, my name is E.L. Staley. I am writing this book first, to bring glory to God our heavenly Father, Jesus Christ our Redeemer, and the Holy Spirit, our Comforter.

This book is about how the devil has tried to destroy me before I came into the saving knowledge of Jesus the Christ. It is about God's call upon my life. This book will reveal God's love, mercy and patience that He not only extended to me, but to you also. It will also reveal heart-aches I suffered as a young boy growing up trying to figure out what life was all about. God was with me from day one, and all through my life, I just didn't know it. Eventually He would reveal to me His revelation of His, "Judgments of America", for our sins against Him.

Growing up in Honey Grove, Texas, where I was born, and in Oklahoma City, and Kansas City, MO, things seemed normal, until I started having problems with my name. I was told that E.L. was not a name and I would get into fights about my name. I was laughed at and ridiculed for not having a regular name like my friends. I didn't tell my parents about my problem, but I would lie awake at night and cry and wonder why my mom and dad named me, E.L. Even into adulthood I had a problem with my name.

I was born left handed. Some of my teachers would beat my hand with a ruler trying to make me use my right hand to no avail. I just couldn't use my right hand. Just about all of my classmates were right handed, and I wondered why I had been given the privilege of being different. Being treated different because of the color of my skin was still another issue. I thought if there is such thing as a curse, then I must have received a double whammy.

The Lord knows our hurts and our sorrows. Jeremiah 1—5, says, "Before I formed thee in the belly, I knew thee"—Ephesians 1—11 says, "In whom also we have obtained an inheritance, being predestinated according to the purpose of him who worketh all things after the counsel of his own will." God has a purpose for each one of us, but we can not know the purpose until we come to Him through His son Jesus Christ. The first thing the Lord did for me after I surrendered to Him, was to reveal to me my name. One night in Bible study our teacher was telling us that words in the Bible that ended with the suffix, EL, meant of God. The word Bethel, is broken down as, Beth—meaning house, and el—meaning of God, and therefore, House of God. But then He turned and pointed at me and said, "But not this E.L. He had told me what I had been wanting to know, and that was why I had been named, E.L. I still have problems with my name but now it doesn't matter, Praise be to God.

At the age of eight years of age, my mother called me into the house and told me that a nurse was there to examine me. I remember how embarrassed I was as the nurse began to examine me and told my mother that I was born circumcised and didn't need to be circumcised. That didn't mean anything to me until I was born again and came across Genesis 17—10—11.

In this book I hope that it will draw you to the Lord if you don't know Him, and if you know Him, I hope it will draw you closer to Him. Jesus is soon to return and we had better set our houses in order. Repent and be ready to go back with him when He comes. PRAISE BE TO THE LAMB OF GOD...

During the early years of my life, I would spend the summer with my grandmother. My older brothers and sisters were grown and living in other cities. My grandmother was a widow during this time, plus she was a devout religious woman. I had to go to church every time she did and that was all the time. She was a missionary filled with the Holy Ghost. I had to feed the chickens, gather the eggs, feed the pigs, chop wood for the heating and cooking stove...we made our soap from lye and grease. Then we had to go to the cotton field to pick cotton or we would pull or use a hoe to chop the weeds around the growing cotton stalks. I didn't mind the chores that much, it was having to go to church. My friends would be out playing and I would be at church at the prayer band, the sewing circle cutting out patterns to make quilts and bed spreads, or the Y.P.W.W.

Many nights my grandmother would wake me up speaking in tongues and dancing around the room until day break. Sometime she would make me get up with her and most times I'd play like I was asleep. I had six brothers and sisters older than myself and I didn't understand why I had to visit my grandmother every summer and be made go to church. I knew one thing, when I got grown, I would not go to anyone's church every again. One day the farmer we picked cotton for was teaching me to drive a tractor. The tractor was pulling a disc harrow across the field, cutting up the big dirt clods. I was sitting on the tractor hitch, as the farmer was telling me how to keep the tractor straight. The sun was beaming down on my back and as I sat there, I fell asleep. I fell off of the hitch between the tractor and the harrow. He was looking straight ahead while talking to me, but some way, he stopped the tractor with the harrow with it's eight or ten inch sharp discs inches from my body. I never knew how he stopped that quick until I was grown and a Christian myself.

As the years began to pass, and I began to grow up, I began to wonder about life. My dad went off to the army and left me, my mom a younger sister alone. Me and my father never had a father and son relationship. He was a person that kept to himself. He would whip me a lot of times for things I didn't understand. Then he and my mother would start to argue and fight. That was mostly the environment that I grew up in. The family that I grew up around there was little love. I guess I really liked visiting my grandmother because she would take time with me and tell me things I didn't know. Seemed like there was real love for me there. It was the church that I didn't like. I didn't understand what would make her get up in the middle of the night dancing and speaking in tongues. I didn't know according to Ephesians 1-11, in whom also we have obtained an inheritance, being predestinated according to the purpose of Him who worketh all things after the counsel of His own will.

I continued to visit my grandmother during the summer when school was out. By my father being in the military, we traveled to every camp that he was stationed at until he was shipped over seas. In 1945 at age 7, we moved to Kansas City, Kansas. My father was discharged from the army. We lived in Kansas until 1949 and during that time my two younger brothers were born. We moved to Missouri for about a year or two then we moved to Oklahoma City. There were four children in the home, me, my younger sister, and my two younger brothers. My mother got us enrolled in school an even though I was still shy and wanted to stay to myself, we made friends with the kids. I met five boys who lived in my neighborhood and we became pretty close. We loved to go to the woods and explore.

At age 13, my life took a sharp turn and it looked like it was for the worst. I had learned about the devil in church, but had never been bothered by him so I thought...I thought if I left God and the devil alone, they would leave me alone. I didn't know there was no neutral ground, that you either served God or you served the devil. I didn't know that all the things that I had suffered at the hands of other people, "For we wrestle not against flesh and blood, but against principalities, against powers, against the rulers of the darkness of this world, against spiritual wickedness in high places", Ephesians 6-12. The devil was trying to destroy me before I came into the saving knowledge of our Saviour, Jesus Christ.

My life truly belong to the Lord because He spared my life too many times...Jeremiah:31-3, "Yea, I have loved thee with an everlasting love, therefore with loving-kindness have I drawn thee." It all started one cold winter day when my close friend went walking thru the old fairgrounds and came upon a frozen lake. He found the bow of a boat sticking out of the ice. We went to see if we could break the ice and get the boat out. We walked out onto the ice to the bow. As we were examining the boat, the ice cracked, and into the cold water we fell. Panic stricken, we held onto the bow to keep from sinking. It had gotten dark when we finally made it to the bank. Scared and cold we knew we couldn't go home like this. We got a fire started some way. We then stripped naked and dried our cloths and then got dressed and went to our homes. That really shook me up because I had heard and read about boys falling into frozen lakes and drowning—I didn't know goodness and mercy was following me.

Winter soon passed, and the next thing I knew it was summer. My friends and I had gotten into lifting weights and I thought I was pretty strong. One hot summer afternoon I was at the swimming pool on North East 4th St. and I remember my grandmother telling me that an idle mind was the devil's workshop. I didn't know what she meant by that. I do now. All the kids were running around the pool having fun, some were swimming. I was sitting on the edge of the pool with my mind a blank. A voice spoke to me and ask me a question, (How long can you hold your breath under water)? I answered the voice, (I don't know?). The voice said, (In the deep end of the pool, there is a drain basin. Why don't you go down and get into it and see how long you can hold your breath.) My friend was playing with the little girls and I called to him and we dove to the bottom of the pool and found the drain basin. We came back to the surface and I told him what I planned to do. There was a steel grate covering the basin and it was just deep and wide enough for me to crouch down inside of it. He was to go down with me and help me remove the grate, go to the surface for some air and come back and help me remove the grate for me to escape.

We dove to the bottom again and it took both of us to lift the steel grate. I got over into the basin and he and I slid the grate over the hole then he went to the surface. I could see his feet kicking in the water above as he held onto the edge of the pool. He didn't come back. As I crouched in the hole, I said to myself, that's all right. I can get out of here by myself. My lungs began to hurt as they began to run out of air...I said it's time to get out of here. I grabbed the grate over my head and pushed upward and it felt like someone had nailed it down. My heart began to pound so loud I could hear it in my ears. I tried it again.

This time with every ounce of strength I had. It wouldn't budge. My heart pounding louder and louder as I said to myself, I'm going to drown. Just then a still small voice spoke and said, (Try it again.) The fear left me and I put my shoulder to the grate one more time and before I could exert any strength, the grate lifted up from the basin and I swam toward the surface as hard as I could with a desperate need to inhale. About halfway to the surface I had to inhale. I inhaled deep through my nose and my mouth. Then and there I should have drowned but to my amazement I inhaled nothing but air. Praise be to my God. I didn't know it was God then because as far as I knew I didn't belong to God neither did I know Him.

St. Luke 6-35...says, For He is kind unto the unthankful and to the evil. As soon as my head broke the surface of the water back into the beautiful sun light a voice spoke to me and said, (That wasn't a miracle. You still had some air left in your lungs.) Even though I couldn't forget what had happened, I believed the devils lie until I got saved and the Lord revealed to me what really happened.

On another occasion at the same pool, I was in the dressing room taking a shower getting ready to get into the pool. The drains in the floor were stopped up and there was about two or three inches of water covering the floor. I stepped out of the shower and walked to the doorway. Still dripping water and standing in water I grabbed both sides of the doorway and leaned out to see if I could see my friends. There was a light switch there with out a cover and I stuck my fingers into that switch. There was a loud cracking sound and blue and red fire and smoke shot from my fingers and feet. I was knocked unconscious. When I opened my eyes, I was lying on my back in the water and a crowd of people were staring down at me asking me if I was all right. I sat up, checked my self and found no burns or injuries. I was however still shaking from the jolt that I had received.

Trembling, I went out to the pool and began to swim. I began to feel sick and decided I needed to go home and rest. I climbed out of the pool and headed to the dressing room. When I got to the doorway, I was feeling pretty weak so I grabbed the inside of the doorway to pull myself in and stuck my fingers into the same light switch. There was a loud cracking sound and I was thrown back out of the doorway. This time I wasn't knocked unconscious but I had to lay there awhile. I sat up and checked myself and once again I found no burns or injuries. After I made it into the dressing room, I couldn't hardly dress myself I was trembling so. I felt like this just wasn't my day.

There was a river northeast of Oklahoma City, about forty or fifty miles that we loved to go to. The river running through rocks, produced foam that looked like soap suds floating up into the sky that you could see for miles. Up stream the water was real muddy and it was said that three or four people had drowned there. Some places it was about four feet deep and other places it was ten or twelve feet. Because of the hidden rocks under the water, they had dived in off of the bluff and broken their necks or crushed their skulls. I didn't' understand why no one had died from all the water moccasins and gar fish I could see swimming in the water.

This day the sky was a pretty blue without any clouds at all. The sun was high in the sky and such a beautiful day. We were standing on the bank watching the gar fish rise to the surface and the cotton mouth water moccasins swim thru the water, when three of my friends dived into the water and swam to the other side. That left one friend and myself on this side. They began to yell to us to swim across. With fear gripping my heart, I dived in. My friend yelled, wait for me and dived in on top of me and pushed me to the bottom of the river. As I tried to push off the bottom of the river, something had my ankle. Panic stricken, I could feel the snakes and gar fish and other creatures I know were there all around me. I'm going to drown I thought.

My heart was pounding in my chest and at that moment a voice spoke and said (Take your time and unwound the barbed wire from around your ankle.) The fear left and I sat down on the muddy bottom of the river and felt my ankle and sure enough there was a piece rusty barbed wire wrapped around my ankle. That day I got a taste of hell without the fire. Even though it was a beautiful day with the sun shinning brightly, under the water it was pitch black dark. I could sense the other creatures all around me but the sweet sounding voice had chased away the fear. I did as I was commanded and unwound the barbed wire from around my ankle and swam to the surface. As soon as my head broke the surface of the water, I could see and hear my friends screaming and crying because they thought I had drowned. As soon as they saw me, they waded into the water to help me out. They wanted to know what had happened to me and I told them that I had gotten a little tied up and I was more than ready to go home.

Not too long after that, one of my close friends came over to my house early in the morning and woke me up saying he wanted to go to the river. He had never come to my house that early and it made me mad. I got out of bed and got dressed. As I tried to make up my bed, he was so close behind me that every time I would turn or backup I'd step on his foot or almost kiss him. I was really getting angry. I wondered why he was all over my back and all in my face and he had never been like this before. A voice spoke to me and said, (You ought to hit him because he's all over you.) Immediately another voice spoke and said, (Don't). I didn't. Finally we met up with the rest of our little band and headed for the river, our favorite pass time.

After that muddy water had run through all the rocks, down stream the water turned crystal clear. The water was bout five or six inches deep and you could see the fish swimming. The other boys had walked ahead of me and my friend that had come to my house early that morning. He was still real close to me, when all of a sudden before I had a chance to even scream, I stepped into a quicksand hole and was sucked down up to my chest. I just had time to grab my friend's ankle to keep me from being sucked under. He looked down with astonishment and grabbed my hand at the same time screaming at our three other friends to come and help. It took all four of them to pull me free. The devil tried to get me angry enough to strike him so he would leave my side and that would have been that, my end. God had sent him early that morning commanding him to stay by my side and he had obeyed.

I started to wonder what was going on. Why these things were happening to only me and not to my friends. Not that I wanted any thing to happen to them. After all we were together all the time.

In St. John:10:10 satan is depicted as, (the thief cometh not, but for to steal, and to kill, and to destroy.) He will kill and destroy your very life and soul if he can. When we die, the flesh returns to the earth but the soul of man which is the real you, will spend eternity either with God the Father or with the devil in hell. The devil was trying to destroy me at every chance he got but God was right there to protect me. I love the Lord with all my heart and there's nothing I won't do for Him.

On this particular sun shinny day, the boys and myself were exploring the woods and every fence we would come to, I would either raise it up or hold it down so they could go under or over it. We had crossed several wire fences, when we came to a large plowed field. As we started across the field, we were walking abreast of each other laughing and talking. Right in my path there was a new stick about an inch wide and about two feet long, and I just bent over and picked it up. We walked until finally we came to the back side of the field. When we got there, there was a barbed wire fence and as I had done in the past, I used the stick and held the fence down and they went across and I went across. We arrived at the pond that we were looking for. We spent two or three hours there and then headed home. We decided to follow the fence to the road. As we walked along the fence, I noticed the fence vibrating and wondered why. Finally we reached the road and the end of the fence. As we stood and watched the fence vibrating, I noticed a wire running from the fence to the telephone pole next to it. It was an electrified fence. God knew that when we got to the fence that I would grab the fence and be shocked. I really didn't attribute finding that stick to God, I just thought I was lucky. It wasn't until after I got saved, and giving God the praise, that I thought what an awesome God He is. He knew the exact path that I would walk that day, and where did He get the stick from, and how did He get the stick out in the middle of the field. As I'm writing this book and remembering what He did, the tears well up in my eyes as I think of how He followed me around protecting me from the evil one. He's precious in my soul.

On another occasion we were out in the woods and came upon a strip-pit mine. Whatever had been mined, had left a deep pit that had filled with water. The boys wanted to go swimming and began to strip off their cloths. I just stood there and watched them. I wasn't in a swimming mood that day. They got into the water and noticed I was still dressed and began to call me chicken, telling me I was scared. They wanted to swim to the other side, which didn't look that far away. So I took my clothes off and got in the water and started to swim to catch up with them. When I looked up to see if I had caught them, they were going back to the bank. I looked ahead of me and was more than halfway across. I said since I'm this close to the other side, I might as well go on. I got to the other side and panic struck my heart. The bank was smooth mud, straight up 10 to 15 feet. There was no rocks or vegetation to grab or anything to hold onto. I'm trying to grab the bank and I'm slipping under the water. I'm too tired to go back. I know I won't make it. I said to myself, E.L. you are going to drown for sure this time. With my heart pounding so loud, it sounds like it's out my chest and in my ears. A voice speaks and says (Start back and when your arms get too tired, take a deep breath and drift down into the water and let your arms rest and them swim until they get tired again.) The fear left and I began to swim back to where the boys were. They were screaming from the bank because they knew I was in trouble. My arms felt like they had bricks tied to them and ached and hurt so bad. I took a deep breath and began to sink down into the dark water. It was warm on the surface, but as I began to drift down into it, it started to get real cold and I would come to the surface and start to swim again. I performed this procedure three or four times until I finally reached the bank. The Lord has saved me literally so many times, that truly my life belongs to Him.

One beautiful day I was on the play ground of the school that my baby sister and baby brothers and I attended, flying a kite. I had a spool of string attached to the kite that I had payed out, and a voice spoke and said, (Add another spool.) I sent my friend to the store and bought another spool and added it to the string and payed it out. The voice spoke again and said (Add another spool.) I sent and bought another spool and added it to the string and payed it all out. By this time the kite was pretty high in the sky. The voice said, (Add more string) and I sent and bought more string and tied it on and payed it all out. By this time the kite was just a speck in the sky. Once again the voice said, (Add more) and I did. When I looked for my kite, it had vanished out of sight. The string ran along the ground for about twenty feet then up into the sky and vanished. Even though I couldn't see the kite, there was a strong pull on the string. Every now and then I would feel the kite tugging on the string and then it would stop. Finally the string went slack and I knew my kite was gone. I couldn't understand why I had added all that string to my kite and lost it. I thought it had been my mind that told me to do it. I didn't realize until after I was saved that it was God.

What He was teaching me was even though I couldn't see the kite, I knew it was still attached to the string because every now and then I could feel the kite tugging on the string. By that experience He was teaching me that even though I couldn't see Him, I would know that He was still with me because every now and then I can feel His tug upon my heart. The Spirit will come upon me and the tears, for no reason, will start to fall. The joy will be unexplainable and the praises will began to issue forth...St. Matthew 28-20, Jesus Himself speaking, said, (Lo, I am with you always, even unto the end of the world.) I have to take Him at his word and trust Him even when things are difficult.

The year is 1950 and I've had my twelfth birthday. At this point I've began to notice the girls, but I'm too shy to talk to any of them. One night I was on my way to the little store down the alley from our house to buy some candy. As I walked down the dark alley, I heard someone snicker. I stopped and looked around but saw no one. Just then about four or five girls jumped out of the bushes and began to wrestle with me. They wrestled me to the ground and began to try and undress me. Screaming and fighting to keep my clothes from being taken off, they were wild and laughing and giggling all the while. About the same time my friend had come by my house and my mother told him that I had gone to the store and he had followed me. He came upon this scene to my rescue and it took both of us to fight them off. I was never more glad to see him. I wasn't mad, I was just scared and embarrassed. I knew these girls. They lived in the neighborhood and I had no idea they would do such a thing. I was just too shy of girls.

I had problems with people, kids and what I considered problems with girls, most of my life but I had began to adjust to it. The thing that happened to me next nearly destroyed me. I had started Jr. High School in the seventh grade making straight a's and b's. I hadn't given my teachers or anyone any problems at school. Many times I would finish my work first and my home room teacher would have me to check the students papers, prepare test papers, even teach or watch the class while he was away. I finished the seventh grade and passed on to the eighth grade. In the first semester of the eight grade, I was on my way to one of my classes when a student in the seventh grade whom I really didn't know, stopped me and told me he had something to show me in his locker. He was so insistent that I went to his locker to see what he had to show me. He opened his locker slightly and I looked in. There was a fifth of wine in his locker and I was shocked when I saw it. I ask him what in the world are you doing with that and he just grinned. I looked around to see if anyone else knew what he had. As I turned, there was my home room teacher standing there, and took us both to the office. This young man told my teacher that he and I had bought the wine.

I told my teacher the truth of what had happened and he took the word of the young man above mine. My world fell in on me. I wasn't expelled by my parents had to come to the school. I didn't know but a handful of the students and only the teachers that I attended their classes, but I found out the whole school knew who I was. The news of what had happened went through the school like wild fire. I would walk down the hall or go to the lunch room, or where ever I went, the kids would start to talk and point and say, there goes Staley, he was caught with some wine. The teachers would stop teaching class and point and tell their class, there goes Staley he was caught with some wine. The other young man's name wasn't mentioned. I was put on display and couldn't understand what was happening.

I tried to live the embarrassment of the ordeal down, but they wouldn't let it die. Before the end of the first semester, I left school. The part that really hurt was that my home room teacher didn't believe me.

During the sixth grade, my friend and I were leaving school when we stopped to watch some majorettes practicing after school and we stopped to watch them. One the girls that I didn't know stole my heart and before I realized what I was saying I told my friend that was the girl that I was going to marry. He looked at me and laughed me to scorn and said you don't even know her, and I said I know it. After about two or three weeks my sister, who was in her room, introduced us. Before we had a chance to get to know one another she moved and I didn't see her any more. I didn't know where she moved to and I didn't think that I would see her again. Well my mother told me we were going to move and we began to pack. We moved into a down stairs duplex and worked thru the night getting the apartment straight. The next morning as I was coming out of my front door on my way to school, I heard some girls talking beside the house. I peeped around the corner of the house and to my most pleasant surprise there was my sister talking to someone coming down the stairs from the apartment above. It was her...we had moved in the apartment below her. I was still shy and didn't talk much but I had to, in a very awkward way, let her know that she had stolen my heart. We began to court up to the time that I quit school.

After I left school I began to spend a lot of time by myself in the woods. I didn't know what I was going to do. I would climb atop the oil derricks as they pumped oil and lie down on the piece of equipment that pumped up and down and go to sleep. Some time I would climb the tallest tree just to sit there and look down on a world that treated me so cruel. Some times while up there, a thunder storm would come up and began to cause the trees to bend and bow while raining. I would stay up there and fall asleep until the storm passed and the trees stopped swaying. I began to prefer animals to people. I began to go on rattlesnake hunts that were held in the hills of Oklahoma. I would catch four or five diamond backs and bring them home. Word began to get out that I had gone crazy because I would be seen around town with diamond back rattle snake around my neck. I was just lost and didn't know what to do. I began to walk the streets drunk crying.

At age 14 my sister came out school and got married. By my sister and the girl up stairs were best friends, Betty which was her name, wanted to get married. We got married and to this union three sons were born.

Without an education things were pretty hard. I would go hunting quite a bit to help supplement our food, plus a good excuse to get out into the woods by myself. On this occasion I was hunting squirrels and been in the woods and was on my way back to the car. As I came out of the woods, I had to walk thru some low grass to get to the road. I had on some moccasins and as I raised my foot walking, a voice spoke and said, (before you put your foot down, look down.) I stopped in my tracks and looked down and laying in the grass right where I would have stepped was a copperhead snake. I didn't see him and I would have stepped on him and I was miles from town. Praise God.

I had several jobs and one of those was at a candy factory. I didn't' work there long. My job was to pick up the finished product and take it down to the store room or take orders such as sugar, spices, flavorings to make the candy to the different floors. This day I had a flat of boxed bonbons I had picked up from about the fourth floor. When the elevator got to the third floor, it started to drop like a ton of bricks. I tried to stop it but nothing worked. It dropped all the way to the basement and bounced back to the first floor. The lights were knocked out. Most of the boxes of candy were bursted open and I was knocked to the floor in the midst of all the candy...Everyone came running over to see if I was all right. I was shaken up but I was all right. A few days later the same thing happened and that's when I quit.

One day I was working on my car in the front yard. I had a 1948 Buick Roadmaster and had the front end jacked up on a jack. As I started to slide under the car on my back a voice spoke and said, (Take that pop case with you.) There was an old Pepsi wooden pop case just laying there and I slid it under the care with me. I stood it up on its side beside my head. It was about five inches higher than my face. As I started to work on the car, I heard a loud crash and the car fell off of the jack down on to the pop case with the frame of the car inches from my face. My wife and mother came screaming out of the house to the car. I couldn't move. I lay there staring at the frame and the big straight eight engine inches from my face. I couldn't even tell them I was all right. I finally got enough strength to tell them I was all right. Finally I crawled out from under the car and they hugged and kissed me glad I was all right.

I had just turned 16 and Betty was 14 when we got married. Our first son was born in 55, our second son was born in 57 and our third son was born in 60. Betty was a quiet, gentle, sweet woman. Our marriage was on the verge of divorce because of me getting drunk and staying out late at night.

One night Betty and I decided to go to one of the night clubs because all of our friends had gone to a dance. When we arrived at the club it was empty. We had forgotten everyone had gone to the dance. I had parked the car across the street from the club and walked over to the club and found it empty. By that time cars began to pull up and park because the dance had just let out. Standing in front of the club watching the people gather, I noticed my wife and her male cousin surrounded by the people. I started across the street to see what was going on. I pushed thru the crowd to the side of my wife just as her cousin slashed the throat of one of three men he had argued with. All three men had been sitting on the window sill of the building where their car was parked at the curb. The second man grabbed the first man which was the one cut and headed for the car. The third man headed for the drivers side of the car. Everyone had scattered to safety. I turned to see if my wife was safe and when I turned back around to see what the men were doing, the man in the back seat stuck his arm out of the window with a pistol aimed at my face and fired five or six times as they drove away.

I was standing about five feet away from the car. The fire from the pistol blinded me and I could hear the bullets ricocheting off the building behind me. It happened so fast I didn't' have time to run, holler or anything. As they sped down the street, with me rubbing my eyes trying to regain my sight, I heard someone behind me, behind the building call my name and say, I'm hit. It was Betty's cousin. He had been shot one time in the chest. The people began to gather to see who had been hit. Betty and I helped her cousin into the car and headed for the hospital. When we arrived he had passed out from internal bleeding. We panicked and I picked him up in my arms and carried him into the emergency room. Him weighing close to three hundred pounds. The doctors said the bullet had punctured his lung and they had to operate on him right then. As Betty and I sat in the waiting room, my mind began to retrace the events that had taken place earlier. I could see the bullets in the chamber and the fire shoot out of the barrel every time he fired. I knew I was too close for him to miss me and hit Betty's cousin, who was hiding behind the corner of the building. He could have hit me with a blindfold on. My head should have been blown off. Betty and I must have been thinking the same thing as we began to cry and embrace one another, tears streaming down our faces. I knew I should've been dead. God's power, grace and his love for me even though I didn't attribute this as God's work. Believe me when I say there's nothing God can't do. I'm not saying something I've heard, I'm telling you something I know. I hear Him saying to you right now, (Behold, I stand at the door, and knock: If any man hear My voice, and open the door, I will come in to him, and will sup with him, and he with Me.)...Revelation 3-20. After I got saved, I use to wonder why these things had happened to me. Part of the reason is for you to know the power, the grace and the love God has for all of mankind.

(O give thanks unto the Lord: call upon His name, make known His deeds among the people. Sing unto Him, sing psalms unto Him: Talk ye of all His wondrous works.) Psalm. 105-1&2. The devil didn't want me to write this book. He put the thoughts that no one will read your book, all the work that's involved and you don't have the time nor the money.

I got a job at the Oklahoma Medical Research Foundation as a custodian. They had a wing in the building with terminally ill people. One day I had finished my work and was sitting in the little office of my supervisor when a voice spoke and said, (Go to the chapel.) The chapel was in the back of the wing for the relatives of a love one who had passed. I got up, not knowing what reason I was to go there. I walked into the chapel and it was empty. I stood there and looked around the room and spotted an organ. I don't play any instrument but I have an ear for music. I can tell when an instrument hits an off key or when someone is singing off key. I sat down at the key board and began to play with the keys. By me not knowing how to play I didn't stay there long and I left. The next day after I had finished my work, the voice spoke and told me the same thing as the day before. I got up and went to the chapel and began to play with the organ. That day I began to get some chords together and after awhile I left. The next day, (Go to the chapel.)

Then I started to go there every day after I finished my work. One day I was back there playing real softly, and heard someone crying. I turned and saw some people in the back of the chapel weeping and I stopped playing but they wanted me to continue. Pretty soon there were more people coming in to hear me play whatever it was they thought I was playing. I got familiar with some of their faces and when I would miss a face I would ask someone where they were and they would tell me they had passed during the night. I would see new faces come in and join the group. Sometimes I would be late going to the chapel and they would come and get me.

I didn't understand what was happening until after I got saved. But God in His tender mercies and great love was ministering to these dying souls thru a person who couldn't play and really didn't know what was happening, but obeyed.

But the natural man receiveth not the things of the spirit of God: for they are foolishness unto him: neither can he know them, because they are spiritually discerned...I Corinthians 2-14. The works of an omnipotent God in this book is most precious to me because I didn't know Him. But He was working wonders in and thru my life. My life was in a turmoil but every time I would hear the voice, I obeyed and later find out it was God.

I met a young lady at the Foundation with terminal leukemia from the Middle East. She and I were about the same age. This young lady knew she was dying, and yet she was full of life. We would walk the hall and talk and she was full of joy and her face would light up when she laughed. One day I came to work and didn't see her. About two days later when I saw her, she was in a wheelchair and one of her legs had been amputated. She was still the same jolly, happy person. About a week or so later her other leg was amputated and she was still the same sweet person. I wept and cried for her my heart breaking. This young lady had made a great impact on my life. I knew this young lady had something I didn't have. She wasn't afraid of dying neither did it bother her to lose both of her legs. One morning I came to work and didn't' see her and inquired about her and was told she passed during the night. I went off to myself and wept for I felt as if part of me had died also.

It wasn't long after that, that I left the job. My marriage was going downhill and with encouragement of those around her, Betty told me she didn't love me any more and wanted a divorce. That finished tearing my world down. I didn't care if I lived or died. About this time my grandmother moved to Oklahoma City and my family had moved to Kansas City. I went and told my grandmother about Betty and I, and that I was going to Kansas City. My grandmother told me to come into the house that she wanted to pray for me because God had something He wanted me to do. I obeyed her against my will and followed her into the house. In my mind I was wondering what could God have for me to do. My wife has just told me she was getting a divorce, I'm going to Kansas City and don't know if I'll ever see her or my sons ever again. I'm a drunk, everyone has turned their backs on me, I've lost my job, what in the world could God have for me to do. I don't even know Him.

My grandmother had me to get on my knees beside her and told me clap my hands and tell the Lord, thank you. In my mind, I'm thinking, my world has fallen apart and you want me to tell Him, thank you, for what. I began to clap my hands and tell the Lord, thank you. Even though I didn't know why. We had been on our knees about two hours and my knees were hurting, my mouth was bone dry, and my arms felt like they were coming out of the sockets. My knees and arms were hurting so bad that in my mind I thought, nothing is happening. I'm getting up from here. No sooner as I thought that in my mind, my grandmother stopped praying and said, don't you get up from here. That really shook me up and I thought, how did she know I was about to get up. I stayed on my knees thanking the Lord until I couldn't stand it any longer and had to get up. This time she didn't say anything but got up with me still praying. I let my arms fall to my side as I watched her pray. All of a sudden something hit me in the top of my head and I looked up at the ceiling and saw nothing. I began to feel something like hot oil or syrup running down my head. It was running real slow.

As whatever it was reached my eyes, felt like boiling hot tears began to issue forth from my eyes. As it reached my mouth, I began to speak in tongue and I know it wasn't me in control of my speaking. As it reached my shoulders, my hands began clapping real fast. I'm trying to figure out what is happening because I know something else has control of me. As it reached my stomach, felt like something was alive moving about inside. Felt like I was on fire but there was no flames. When it finally reached my feet, I started jumping up and down dancing. When it had gone to the end of my feet, it started from my head again but this time I was cooling down to normal body temperature. I cooled down all the way down to the tips of my toes. My grandmother stood praising God all the while this was happening and as soon as I had cooled down to my toes, she spoke and said God has baptized you with the Holy Ghost and He has something for you to do. I was really confused as I just stood there and looked at her as she stood smiling at me.

She told me that the Lord had told her to go on the evangelist field. That was next to the last time I saw her. I went out to a club and got drunk. The next day I told her I was leaving for Kansas City. After I went to Kansas City, the Lord called her home. I went down to the bus station and bought a ticket to Kansas City and boarded the bus. My heart was torn in so many pieces that I felt I was about to die. The bus pulled out of the station and hit the highway. By the time it got to the city limits, it was just getting dark and the people had settled down for the long ride. I was sitting about middle ways the bus and had let my seat back to try and go to sleep, when a voice said, (E.L.) It was so loud I knew everyone on the bus heard it. I stood up and looked toward the back of the bus and everyone was sleep. I looked up front and no one was looking back at me and so I sat back down. I thought that some one was playing games with me but no one ever came to me.

That was the longest saddest ride of my life. I felt like I had been sentenced to a life of pain, sadness and rejection. The bus finally reached Kansas City and I caught a cab to my mother's house. Everyone was glad to see me and we hugged and kissed one another. My mother told me that there was an apartment next to hers and that I could go next door and get some rest. I agreed. I entered the bedroom and lay down on the bed on my back with my hands under my head. I was laying there wondering, what am I going to do, as well as thinking about the experience with the Holy Ghost, and who it was that had called my name out loud. The sun was shinning thru the window as I lay on the bed. All of a sudden two big invisible hands gripped my biceps and pinned me to the bed. I started screaming but nothing came out of my mouth. I could feel the hands and the fingers as I struggled to get free. It held me for a minute or so, then let me go. I just about tore the screen door off its hinges. I ran to my mother's apartment and told them what had happened. They laughed me to scorn. I was sorry I had told them.

After they finally stopped laughing, my mother told me that I had feel asleep and had a nightmare. I stood there looking at everyone and thinking in my mind that maybe they were right. What other explanation was there. I said yes agreeing with them and went back to the room and went in and laid down on the bed. As soon as I put my hands under my head, the hands grabbed me again. I knew I wasn't sleep this time. I screamed but nothing came out. I struggled trying to get free and after about two minutes it let me go and out of the door I went. I ran in my mother's apartment out of breath and scared. I told them there was a ghost over there. Once again they began to laugh at me but I didn't care this time because I knew something had grabbed me. I sat down as they tried to settle me down. I thought about the things that had happened to me in the last week or so and thought maybe I'm loosing my mind.

Before I left Oklahoma City, Betty and myself with the kids had been living with her mother. I would call her long distant wanting to see if we could get back together. Her mother would answer the phone and tell me she didn't want to speak to me. I didn't believe that, but after I could never get to speak to her I thought it must be really over.

The year is 1961 and I've turned 23 years old. I found a job at a restaurant and met my present wife, Evelyn. She had four kids when we met, and soon we began to date. I know God had to have given her to me. She has been faithful to me from day one until the present, 33 years. We moved into a house and started to set up house keeping. I stayed high on alcohol to ease the pain of my separation from my wife. Even though we partied all the time, my heart was still in Oklahoma. Evelyn stayed by my side. We got jobs at the same motel and one day just before Thanksgiving and we wouldn't get paid until after Thanksgiving. I went into work. It was about 6 a.m. and still dark. I went inside and changed into my uniform and had an urge to go back to the car. When I got to the car, I had no reason to return to car so I stood there wondering what I was doing there. It was real cold that morning and as I turned to go back inside, I heard a sound like my radiator was boiling. I looked under the car to see if the antifreeze was running out. There under the engine was a wild duck warming himself by the heat from the engine. I chased him out and it tried to fly but it was to cold. All it could do was run and fly about a few inches above the ground. I finally caught it and put it into a box and when I got off that afternoon, I carried it home. We fed it bread and water and some vegetables, until Thanksgiving and we had duck for Thanksgiving.

I thank God for being always mindful of me when I wasn't mindful of Him.

One evening I had gone to a night club wearing only some slacks, loafers and a thin sport coat. It was winter but the sun was shining and I had rode a city bus to the club. I stayed at the club until closing time just in time to catch the last bus home. When I came out of the club, another blizzard had come up and there was about a foot of snow all ready on the ground. Plus the temperature had dropped to the lower double digits and heavy snow was blowing in. Waiting for the bus, I had gotten real cold by the time it arrived. I boarded the warm bus for the ride home. As the bus drove slowly toward my house, I fell asleep. When I woke up and looked out of the window, I knew I had rode past my street. I thought I had missed it about a couple of blocks, so I got off. When I stepped off of the bus the blowing snow hit me in the face and sort of sobered me up. When I looked around to get my bearing I was at the end of the bus route, some forty blocks or more past my street. The bus had turned around and was headed back to the barn.

The blizzard was blowing in from the north and I had to walk facing the blowing snow. There wasn't another vehicle or soul anywhere in sight. I began walking slipping and sliding falling on my face trying to get home. I don't know how many blocks I had walked, when I began to get real warm and sleepy. I knew I was going to freeze before I got home. Now when I fell, I would curl up in the snow and wait for death to come. I was so cold but yet warm that I just didn't care. A voice began to speak and say, (get up and walk.) I got up and began to walk with the wind and big snow flakes blowing into my mouth and eyes as well as up my nose. I tried walking backwards to keep the snow out of my face, but that didn't help much. The snow was so blinding, that I couldn't tell if I was making any headway. And when I fell, I would curl up in the warm snow to go to sleep, but the voice would tell me to get up and walk and I would obey. My feet and hands felt like they were gone and I was walking on clubs. I don't know how many times the voice commanded me to get up and walk, but the club closed about 1 a.m. and it was about 4 a.m. when I finally made it home. When I did make it to my front door, all I could do was knock on the door with my head. Thanks be to God I suffered no ill effects. I just knew my hands and feet had frozen.

There was the time when my wife wanted me to drive her to the Kansas City, Kansas side to see her brother. We had been riding around drinking and had gotten high and now she wanted to drive across the viaduct which was quite a ways from where we were. I took her but I was mad because he and I didn't' see eye to eye. As I drove across the elevated highway, I drove as fast as the car would go and when we got there. he wasn't home. I did get mad and drove as fast as the car would go to get back home. We went home and went to bed. The next morning, which was Sunday, we got up to go to the bootleg house to buy something to drink. I pull up to the house and parked the car. While we sat there, we felt a bump and I thought someone had parked behind us and had hit my car. When I looked behind us, I didn't see anyone. When I turned around, I saw a tire rolling past my car. That looks like my tire. Sure enough it was my tire and I got out of the car and caught the tire. The bearing in the left front wheel had gone out and the whole wheel came off. I bought a new bearing and some alcohol and some drunk man and myself put the bearing on and we went home. God kept the bearing from coming off as I drove back and forth across the viaduct like a fool. We would certainly have had a nasty situation.

On another occasion I went to this night club that blacks had started to patronize. When I went in, I bought a beer and sat down in a booth alone. There were three white men and three white women sitting at the bar and another black man. The black man finished his beer and left. I guess I should've left with him. The white owner-bartender was talking to these people from behind the bar. They acted like they weren't paying me any attention and I was attending to my own business. The men went out to their vehicles one at a time and returned with a rifle. I thought they were hunters talking about a hunting trip. I got up and went to the men's room and when I stepped out of the rest room, the owner grabbed me in my collar and shoved me up against the pool table. I knocked his hands away and drew my fist back to hit him. At that time I heard all three rifles cocked. I looked back with my fist in midair to see all three rifles aimed at my head. I let him go and he grabbed me in the collar again and pushed me down on the pool table and began to beat me in the face. As he beat me, my tooth penetrated my top lip, both eyes was blackened, nose bleeding, lip bursted, blood running down the front of my shirt. All of a sudden, one of the women began crying and screaming so loud that he stopped beating me and turned to look at her. I raised up and looked at her as the other three men were also looking at her. She was pleading. Don't kill him, please don't, look at him. He's bleeding bad. We all stood there watching her. Then he turned to me and said, get out of here before we kill you. I wanted to go but I was scared. A voice spoke and said, (walk). The fear left and I began to walk to the door. When I reached the door, I turned and looked each one of them in their eyes and turned and walked out into the beautiful sun light. The women that was crying, when I looked into their eyes, I could see the hurt as well as the compassion she had for me. I have never seen such hatred in a person as I seen in those men. The woman was my ram in the bush.

As I stood there on the sidewalk, a voice began telling me how they beat Jesus all night long and how they plucked His beard out, punched Him in the face, how He was spat upon, and humiliated, lied on and then crucified Him. Tears began streaming down my face. At the same time I'm wondering what does that have to do with me. Another thing I couldn't understand is I wasn't drunk or even high, and yet I felt no pain during the attack. Neither after the attack and I wasn't angry. I started walking toward home rejoicing in me soul. I met my brother who was always looking for trouble and asked, man what happened to you. I told him what had happened and he wanted to go back and blow the place up but I said no. He didn't know what to think about me. I met a couple of black panthers and they wanted to go back and get even. But I said no. They didn't know what to think about me. When I walked in my house and Evelyn saw my face she began to cry. I went to the mirror and looked and I was a sight. Both eyes were swollen shut. I had a hole in my upper lip, plus both lips were bursted and swollen and I was bloody.

I was completely confused because I didn't know the Lord as my personal Savior and I wasn't living for Him. Every time I would go to a party at one of our friends house, when Evelyn and I walked in, they would say here comes the preacher, and I would get very upset and tell them I was not a preacher and don't call me that anymore. Many of our friends had girl and boy friends on the side. Every time I would try, I would be exposed right away. I would try lying and get caught and it would be so embarrassing.

One day I went into a grocer store to cash my payroll check. I walked up to the window and laid my check on the counter, under the glass window. The man behind the glass saw me standing there and picked up a invoice and started to read it. He left the booth and went back into the store room out of sight. I got angry because I thought he had saw me standing there. As I started to reach and get my check, right by my check was a large stack of money. I looked behind me to see if anyone was there. No one was. Couldn't anyone see me standing there. When I turned back around to where my check and the money was, a voice spoke so loud that I just knew that everyone in the store heard it and knew who it was speaking to. It said, (Thou shalt not steal). It scared me so bad that I grabbed my check and ran from the store.

It got so that every time that I did something wrong, I got caught. My friends would date for years and not get caught. They could do what so ever they wanted to and not get caught. One day I thought in my mind, Lord why are you on my case when I don't belong to you? I would not speak it with my mouth. I didn't know that Psalm 139...1&2...says, O Lord Thou has searched me, and known me. Thou knowest my downsitting and mine uprising: Thou understandest my thought afar off. Verse...5...Thou hast beset me behind and before, and laid thine hand upon me...

According to Psalm 89...1...I will sing of the mercies of the Lord forever, with my mouth will I make known thy faithfulness to all generations:

Psalm 89...6...For who in the heaven can be compared unto the Lord? Who among the sons of the mighty can be likened unto the Lord?

Romans 5...20...Moreover the law entered, that the offense might abound. But where sin abounded, grace did much more abound: ...What the scripture is saying is, the law or the commandments of old came to show that there was sin in man and he could not keep the law. But where there was great sin, there was much more love and forgiveness...

One night Evelyn and I had been over to some of our friends house drinking, and had gotten drunk. We started home, but I was so drunk that she had to drive. She didn't have drivers license but I let her drive because I couldn't see. It was early about 3 in the morning when we heard a siren and flashing red lights flashed in our back glass. Evelyn pulled to the curb and before the police got to the car, I told her to change seats with me. The police had us to get out of the car and asked us where we were going and we told them, home. I told them I was driving and to let my wife go and to take me on to jail. They asked us where we had been and we told them. Once again I told them to let my wife go and take me to jail. The officer asked me why was I anxious to go to jail. I told him I wasn't, but I knew that's where I was going, but let my wife go. He told us to get in his car and his partner got in our car and off we went. We sat in the back seat wondering who we would get to bail us out of jail. As we neared the street where we should have turned to get to the police station, the officer kept going. In the back seat whispering, maybe their taking us to a different station. When we looked out of the window to see where we were, we were at home. The officer pulled up behind us in our car. We couldn't believe what was happening. The other officer parked our car and the officer we were riding with told us to get out of the car and for us not to touch our car until we had sobered up. We still couldn't believe it. We thanked both of the officers and then went into our house. The officers sat there for a few minutes, then they left.

If you have been in similar situations or whatever problems you've had and have gotten out of them in ways that you didn't understand, it was God. For a long time I thought I was lucky or I thought I had handled the situation well.

Right now God wants you to know that He loves you more than you'll ever know and that He wants to be Lord of your life. Whether you know it or not or if you'll ever realize it, but He died just for you. Praise Him. I love Him.

The year is 1966, and I've had my 28th birthday and two daughters added to the family. One in 64 and one in 65. The family now numbers 8.

As time goes by, we are still throwing parties and getting drunk with our so-called friends. Things had stayed the same as far as our finances were concerned. We were still struggling just to make ends meet. I had seen my sons only about three times since Betty and I separated. Betty had started a new life and I didn't want to cause any problems. I still had some pain and angry in my heart.

I had always wanted an electric train set when I was a kid but my parents weren't able to buy me one. I'm 56 years old and I am still fascinated with trains. The year is 1971 and I'm at work on the graveyard shift when I receive a call from Evelyn saying she and the police had gone to her father's house and found him dead. I told her that I would be right there. When I arrived, they had already taken the body away. We searched the house for documents and other valuables. She told me there were several items she wanted to take home before she and her brother got rid of the stuff. I went and rented a trailer and backed up to the house. One of the items she wanted was a chest type freezer that she said her father had bought when she was a little girl. Evelyn and I and a neighbor found the freezer on the back porch. When we attempted to load it on the dollie that we had, we couldn't budge it. It was so heavy. We searched the house and finally found the key for it. When we opened the freezer, it was packed to the brim with electric trains, track, buildings and controls all wrapped in newspaper. I couldn't believe my eyes. We packed the trains in boxes so we could move the freezer. I was very excited and couldn't hardly wait to get home to unwrap the trains to see what was there.

When I got everything unwrapped, there was enough engines and cars to have about seven or eight complete trains with six or seven cars to each train. That began to consume my time and I built a layout that covered half of my basement. I built a small city with lit buildings, trees, people, cars, bridges and streets. There were passenger and freight trains. That kept my mind occupied for a few years.

We finally moved into a better house and I rebuilt a bigger and better city. One night I had been drinking and didn't have driver's license, no tags on my car when I had a wreck. I was cited for being drunk, wreckless driving, and no tags. I knew I was in trouble and didn't know what I was going to do. I got me a lawyer, and he told me I was in trouble but he would do what he could. That didn't sound to promising. Court day came and I was real nervous waiting for my lawyer. The people that I had hit came into court with their lawyer and looked at me as if to say, You've had it. Court started and my lawyer still hadn't showed up. I really got nervous. They called my name and we all went before the judge. I stood there with my head down as they read the charges. I knew I was guilty and was ready to except my punishment. I stood there and thought my lawyer had betrayed me by not showing up. When they were finished reading the charges, the judge said not guilty. The lawyer for the people I hit said but your Honor. The Judge said it again. Case dismissed. I slowly raised my head to look at the judge and what a surprise, The judge was my lawyer. The reason I didn't see him come in is because He came in thru the Judges back entrance. I could have kissed him. As I stood there and watched him in utter shock wondering how did this happen, he looked at me and smiled as I looked at them and then turned and walked out of court.

The year is 1975 and another daughter has been added to the family. It was about this time that I began to have dreams so real that it seemed as if I was actually there. I didn't pay any attention to the dreams at first until they began to come to pass. In the first dream I saw an upper room that was snow white. I saw a snow white casket surrounded by snow white flowers. A breeze was blowing thru an open window with snow white curtains and I heard Mahalia Jackson singing, in the upper room. Not long after that, the Lord called her home. She was one of my favorite gospel singers. I didn't think to much of it. I thought it was just a coincident.

In the next dream I saw trash bags and trash stacked up everywhere and right after the dream, the refuse collectors went on strike in New York and there was garbage bags and trash everywhere. That kind of got my attention as I wondered what's going on?

In the next dream I had, I saw some weeds. A railroad crossing sign and railroad tracks running diagonal across the street. Even though I didn't know where it was, I felt like I knew the place and at the same time I didn't know the place. I wondered how can this be? Either you know a place or you don't. I had a 750 Honda motorcycle and I decided to take a trip to Oklahoma City. I started out riding at the speed limit which was 55 miles an hour. Everybody was passing me like I was doing 20 MPH. I looked at my speedometer and it had 125 on it. I said I'll see what this baby will do. I revved it up to 65, 75, 95, 110, 125. I got over into the passing lane, passing every thing as if they were standing still about three or four miles down the highway, I saw a huge moving van and it began to get bigger and bigger as I closed the distance between him and me. The wind was rushing past, but as I came up about 20 feet behind him, I got in his draft. All of the wind was going over him and I couldn't feel any wind at all. As I shot past him, I came back into the wind. The motorcycle raised vertical upon its rear wheel with its front wheel straight up in the air. I said E.L. this is it. I hit the kill switch and held on for dear life. All I could see was them picking up bits and pieces and trying to explain to Evelyn what had happened. The bike was riding as straight as an arrow and the people passing were waving and clapping and hollering out of their windows telling me ride that bike. They didn't know I felt as if I was about to have a heart attack and was riding for my life. I was looking for the bike to blow over backwards any minute. As I held on, the bike started to slow a little and very slowly the front wheel began to come down. The engine is dead and I'm just coasting along. I rode about a mile before the wheel began to come down. Finally the front wheel touched the ground and I coasted another ¼ of a mile before I started to brake. I brought the bike to a halt, put the kickstand down, stepped off of the bike and collapsed to the ground. My legs were like water. I had to lie there about twenty minutes before I gained enough strength to get up.

Once again God had intervened in my behalf. He's my God and I'm His child. I found my relatives and visited with them awhile and decided to go to the neighborhood where I had lived. When I got there, I parked my bike and walked to where my house use to sit. They had torn all of the old houses down and grass and weeds had grown over the land. As I stood there thinking of my past, I looked down and there was the railroad tracks. I looked and there was the railroad crossing sign. At that moment I felt big burning eyes staring at me from the back. Great fear came upon me. My hair stood on end. Tears watered my eyes and I began trembling so bad I could hardly stand. I knew that God was in that place. The reason that I knew the place was because I use to live there and the reason I didn't know it, was because all the houses had been torn down. Now what I didn't understand as I'm writing this book, God had us to sell our home in Kansas City of 22 years ago and the next thing I knew we were living in our motor home in my daughter-in-law's driveway. Her house is two blocks from the area where I lived thirty some years ago and where the railroad tracks and the railroad crossing sign I saw in the dream. They are still there. I've asked the Lord, what in the world am I doing back here?

The next dream I had was of me and Betty walking down a sidewalk shaded on both sides with trees. I told her, girl there is something I want to tell you. As I walked, she seemed to be floating along as she smiled at me without saying anything. She began to speed up and I had to walk fast to keep up with her. I told her to wait because I wanted to talk to her, but she just got faster. She made it to the corner of the block before I did and turned the corner. When I got there she was gone. I wondered what this was all about. I can't remember how long it was but I received a phone call from my oldest son in Oklahoma wanting me to come and get him and his wife and bring them to Kansas City. I hadn't heard from him since he had gotten grown. Evelyn and I got up and got on the highway headed for Oklahoma. We went to my ex-mother-in-law's house because Betty, her husband, and all of my sons were living there. I walked into the house and spoke to everyone. I hadn't seen these people in about twenty some years. I still hadn't forgot the events that led to our separation. As my son loaded their belongings into the car, I was told that Betty was in the back bedroom. I went back there and she was sitting up in the bed with a smile on her face. I smiled at her and asked her how she felt, and she said fine. I was glad to see her again. I told her it was good to see her again and we hit the highway back to Kansas City. About two days, my son got a call as I came into the room. As he stood there, tears started to fall and then he hung the phone up. He said, Betty is dead. We were all shocked and I said, it can't be because I just talked to the woman. I had to take my son back to Oklahoma. The Lord let me see her one more time before He called her home. That was in 1975. It is hard for us as a people to understand the love and mercy of God because we judge His love and mercy for us, according to the love and mercy we show toward one another. I John 4.10, Herein is love, not that we loved God, but that He loved us, and sent His son to be the propitiation for our sins...

After Betty's death, I began to pay attention to the dreams and I began to have on a regular basis. In one dream, I saw an airplane in the sky turn on it's side and fall into the water, killing the passengers and me pulling someone from the water. Well a short time later an airplane lost it's wing I believe as it turned on it's side and crashed into some water I believe in Washington D.C. I said it's nothing to these dreams because I wasn't there to pull anyone from the water. About a week later, we were at the lake where we kept our pontoon boat and Evelyn wanted to go ashore. I took her to the dock and as she stepped from the boat, she pushed the boat from the dock and fell into the water. As I rushed toward the front of the boat and reached down and grabbed her hand to pull her up onto the boat, I got a chill and my heart skipped a beat. That was the other half of the dream I had about the airplane.

In another dream I saw two caskets sitting side by side and two hearses sitting out side of a funeral home. I had just about forgotten about the dream, when my younger sister and her oldest son were murdered in Oklahoma City. Their bodies were shipped back to Kansas City. As we sat in the funeral home wondering how and why did this happen, I looked at the caskets and my heart skipped a beat. There as in my dream two caskets side by side. After the funeral was over and they carried the caskets out side, there were two hearses parked there, one behind the other. At this point, I knew that God had to have something to do with this but I didn't know why.

The next dream I had I saw a big black ship just sitting out in the water. I'll tell you more about that later on in this book.

At this time I was working for the street department of Kansas City and had started as a laborer shoveling asphalt and had moved up the ladder to become an equipment operator 11, heavy equipment. I operated the back hoe, hi-loader, asphalt rollers, dump trucks and was learning to operate the grader. I had one operation on my lower back where they fused two discs, and they were going to have to operate again. I went into the hospital a few days before the operation to give some blood in case I needed blood, I could receive my own blood. I was lying in a room with two other men and they were putting some fluid back in my body to replace the blood. A doctor came in and said Mr. Staley your iron count is a little low and I'm going to give you some iron. He took a little ampual with something black in it and put it in the fluid bottle hanging there and went out of the room. I laid there and watched the black fluid come down the IV and enter my arm. My bed was such that I couldn't see out in the hallway but the other men could. As the fluid entered my arm, I felt my heart quiver. Just then the code blue alarm went off. I heard people hustling about with equipment. I ask the two men what was going on and they told me somebody was dying. All of a sudden all these nurses and doctors with all these machines rushed into the room. I said to myself, one of these fools is dying and don't even know it. As I lay there watching which bed they would go to, they all rushed around my bed. About that time I felt like someone was tearing my heart out of my chest and I past out. When I regained consciousness, they had all of the machines hooked up to me. I was the fool that was dying, but God said not today I have something for my son to do. They didn't want to tell me but finally told me the iron had gotten into my blood stream too fast and induced a heart attack. It had damaged my heart and I had to stay two days while my heart healed.

I had the operation and was off from work for about a year. After that year I was still unable to go back to work and they told me that I was terminated and workers comp was stopping the money I was receiving. I didn't know what I was going to do. I had about a thousand dollars in the credit union which was my money that I had put in the account and about three thousand dollars in my pension plan. I thought if I can get this money that it will carry us for awhile until I figure out what I'm going to do. I went to the credit union to withdraw my money and the woman came up with some excuse as to why I couldn't get it. I heard a door slam in my ears. I went to the city to get my pension money and once again I was told I couldn't get it at this time. I heard another door slam in my ears. I went home dejected and didn't know where to turn.

I explained to Evelyn what had happened and she tried to console me. As I sat there thinking about hearing those doors slam in my ears, I knew they had been closed for a reason. For the first time I can remember, I said, Lord you're trying to tell me something. What is it. Some time back I had sent the 700 club a donation and they had sent me some tapes. I got some serious problems and Evelyn came in and ask me if I had played the new tape that had come in the mail. I told her no. She came back in the bedroom and said why don't you play it. I was getting angry. The tape player had been lost for quite awhile. Both of us had looked for it. She went right to it and brought it and the tape to me and left the room. I started the tape and sat down on my bed. A voice began to speak that I recognized and it got my attention. I had been in at least twelve situations that could have killed me and the voice reminded me of those twelve times as well as other situations and told me it was Him that had gotten me out of them. It was the Lord speaking directly to me. The fear of what I was going to do about my job left and unspeakable joy began to fill my heart and hot tears began to fall to the floor. I said, Lord if you will forgive this fool I will live the rest of my life for you. I will go where ever you want me to go. I will speak what ever you want me to and to who ever you want me to speak it to. I was rejoicing and praising His name when the tape clicked off. I said let me do this over and rewound the tape and started it over. As the tape started to play, it said, Hello this is Pat Robertson and we are going to talk about such and such to day. I said wait a minute that's not the person that was talking a few minutes ago. I left the room and told Evelyn what had happened. That has been 15 years ago and I've been living all I know for Him.

Just before I surrounded to the Lord, I thought I was about to die. No matter the amount of alcohol I drank I couldn't get drunk. I thought surely I'm about to leave here. I had carried Evelyn to a club to celebrate her birthday. At that time I loved to dance. I would start to dance and everyone would move to their seat or off the dance floor to watch me dance by myself. Sometimes Evelyn and I would be broke and men and women would buy us drinks or give me money for me to dance. This night I had the floor, sliding and gliding, doing the splits and a voice spoke and said, Don't you fell like a fool. I stopped dancing and began looking at all the people that were looking at me. I thought, I do feel like a fool. I'm the only one on this dance floor and I went and sat down. Evelyn asked me what was wrong. All the people began to ask me to come back. I couldn't tell her I was hearing a voice, so I told her I was just tired. As I sat there, another voice spoke and said why did you sit down, look at all the pretty girls begging you to dance. I looked around the room and it was a lot of them. I got up and went back to dancing and when I got to the center of the dance floor the Lord touched my feet and I started tripping over my own feet and fell a couple of times. That really scared me.

Embarrassed and unable to dance, I took my seat and Evelyn asked me, what in the world is wrong with you. Are you drunk or something? I didn't dare tell her my feet are dead as far as dancing goes. I can't pat my feet even in church with out them getting out of beat.

The Lord was really dealing with me and at this point I began to realize it was Him. I didn't think I was worthy of His love and I was unworthy of doing anything for Him. The last thing that happened before I surrendered to the Lord happened this way. I was troubled by all the events that had happened prior to my surrender to the Lord. There was a club a block from our house that was predominantly a black club. One night as I sat at a small table minding my own business, I heard a man's voice say, excuse me, may I sit with you. The rest of these people seem to be prejudice. Now this club was packed with no place to sit. People were standing everywhere. Black people. I looked up and there was a white man in the midst of all these black people asking me if he could sit with me at my little table. I said sure and he sat down. He was a professional over the road bus driver in uniform. He asked me what I was drinking and I said vodka and he bought me a double shot. He wanted to talk and I didn't and I was getting angry. I had let him sit with me but I didn't feel like talking. I've never been a prejudice person. I didn't want to be bothered by anyone. He ask me if I had seen what he was driving. I said no and didn't care what he was driving. He asked me to come out side and see what he was driving. Now I'm really getting angry. Man I don't care what you're driving. He didn't give up so finally I said okay let me see what you're driving. He got happy and we went out side pushing thru all the people to get outside.

It was getting dark and the street lights had come on. Parked at the curb was an eagle over the road bus which is the same as the Trailway busses. It had a beautiful paint job and with all the sparkling chrome and the chrome wheels it was a beautiful bus. I said man that's all right. We went back inside and no sooner had we sat down, that he ask me if I had ever driven a bus before and I said no. He said you can do it, come out side and let me show you how. As I sat there and looked at him, I wondered how did I get this nut case with all these other people in here. I thought either he is crazy are he's trying to set me up. I told him I didn't want to and I didn't want to. Driving his bus was the farthest thing from my mind. I was getting high from the vodka he had bought me. When I told him I didn't want to drive he got real sad. He didn't give up. I became angry and thought that if I say okay, maybe he would say I was just kidding and then drop the subject. I said okay and he got real happy as we went outside to where the bus was parked. To my amazement he opened the door and told me to sit down in the drivers seat. He started up that diesel engine and it rocked the whole bus.

He turned on the lights, told me to push in on the clutch and he released the parking brake then he shifted the bus in gear. As he stood beside me, he told me to ease out on the clutch and we took off. As I looked in the rearview mirror, and saw all that bus and all them seats stretched out behind me, I sobered up in a hurry. All I could think of was, we are going to die, we are going to jail. I held the steering wheel tightly as I maneuvered the bus thru Swope Park. He stood there beside me saying your doing good. I came up the highway from the park and said I wish my family could see me. He asked where are they? I said at home. He said go get them. It seemed like a dream. Like it wasn't really me. I pulled up to the house and my family saw all the lights and heard the airbrakes and looked out and saw this big bus and I waved to them to come on. They all came out of with their mouth wide open trying to figure out what was going on. I took them back thru the park and back home. I had to have some witnesses to tell me I wasn't crazy. He asked me if he could come to my house the next time he was in town and I told him yes. That was the first and last time that I saw him. I surrendered to the Lord right after that.

I'm reminded of Moses when the Lord was about to send him to Egypt to tell Pharaoh to let the children of Israel go. He asked, if the elders should ask who sent me what should I answer. God said, I Am that I Am. Tell them, I Am sent you. God was and is saying, I Am your deliverer, your redeemer, your mother, your father, your husband, your health, your wealth, your friend, your refuge, your heavenly father. God is saying to you that what ever you need in this life and the life to come, He is.

A few weeks after I got saved, Evelyn came to me and told me that one of our younger daughters was pregnant and if they got the money could they get an abortion. I stood there in shock and as I'm pondering this thing in my mind, the Lord spoke so loud out of my mouth, No, that I had to look behind me to see if the indeed He was standing there. It really scared me because I'm still thinking of what I'm going to say. Well both of them got real mad at me and said that I didn't love them and that our daughter was too young to have a baby. They stopped speaking to me. I said Lord you spoke to them out of my mouth and now they're mad at me. He said go to church. We didn't know about any of the churches because I didn't play with God. I looked in the yellow pages under the Churches of God in Christ, and the first one in there, was the one we were going to. Then we would look around until we found a church we wanted to join. We got dressed that Sunday and went to the church I had found in the yellow pages. We still weren't speaking. I sat one side of the church and they sat on the other side.

The service started and the pastor came in about the time for him to preach. I hadn't seen him before, neither did I know him, nor he, us. He came to the pulpit and started to preach and about twenty minutes into his sermon, he stopped in the middle of a sentence and just stood there with a blank look on his face. I said to my self, what's wrong with him. The next thing he said was, you mothers out there who have young daughters that are pregnant, don't kill them babies. Tears began streaming down my face because I knew who it was that put those words in the man's mouth. Evelyn went screaming down to the alter before alter call and gave her life to Christ and joined the church. That meant that I would have to join this church to. I was upset because we were supposed visit other churches before we joined a church. It was God's plan. I met the pastor after the service and joined the church the next Sunday.

I got involved in the church and I know it was nobody but God. God had stopped me from cursing, drinking, chasing women, lying. I mean over night but I had come from a world of people self centered to a world of Christ centered. I felt I needed time to find out what this new life was really about. I was thrust into the ministry before I knew what was going on. I became the teacher for the adult men's class. The van driver, the trustee board, keeping the records of the offerings and tithes, the maintenance man of the church, prayer counselor on the phone, president of the brotherhood, and taking up the offering. Many times I felt like a twig in the Missouri River. The twig doesn't know where the river is carrying it, plus it can't get out of the river.

Our daughter that was pregnant, gave birth to a baby boy and ran off from home. We kept the baby and raised him until he turned 14 years old, which was 94. All the other children are grown and have moved out. Our youngest daughter was still at home and still is, even though she is 19, and thinks she is grown. One of the other daughters had a baby girl, and was putting her up for adoption and we went to see them at the hospital, and the Lord put it on my heart to bring the baby home. She is now 8 years old.

I had two operations on my lower back and had to have another one on my lower back. Then I had to have an operation on my chest and in my neck on my spine. I've had pain in my lower back and neck to this day. I haven't been able to hold but two jobs for a short period of time, from the time I got saved. One of those jobs I received when I was going thru a rehabilitation program after surgery.

My counselor sent me to talk to the founder coordinator of a program for the developmentally disabled. They ranged in age from 18 to 50 years old. Some were born that way, and some were injured someway or other. I went to talk to the man about the job and as we talked, I sat there all nervous and wondering when he was going to ask me for my credentials and experience. He never did. He asked me when I could start, and I said Monday.

There were about six women and two men beside myself. I was the only black. They all had their credentials and scholastic degrees hanging on their walls, and I hadn't even finished Jr. high school. I had to ask myself, what am I doing here. I started with six or seven clients. It was my job to train these people for some kind of job, that they might become self sufficient. I had to keep a chronological report on each client. I had to monitor their medication, and teach them social skills. My area of training was to train them that were capable, to assemble and disassemble small components, by repetition. Others, I trained to stock shelves and to fill orders from the stock room.

They had a 1250 offset printing press that I was to train with. I had never seen a press, let alone operate one. They call a representative from the company that built the press. The lady and I spent one whole day trying to get the press operating with out success. One day the Lord led me to the press and began to show me why the press wouldn't run. I repaired the press and got it running and trained one of my clients so well that he got a job with a government weather bureau. I had to go to the job site to help him get settled in and talk to his supervisor. The man told me he had to meet me because my client had told him some things about the press that he didn't know.

Many of the parents and relatives came to the foundation to meet me. Because all my clients talked about at home was Mr. Staley. One day I sat down and began to assess my progress. I had 27 clients. Things were getting out of hand. The other counselors were getting stressed out, and I would find myself counseling and praying for them. Sometimes they would began to cry because of the work load. One of my clients was seeing demons and said they wanted to kill him. I had prayer with him and the demons left and he got saved. The founder had me to pray for him because he had to have surgery on his leg for a blocked artery. He came thru the surgery and made a miraculous recovery. About a couple of months later a blood clot formed in the artery and was going to need more surgery. I asked him to let me pray for him and he said, I have already had prayer. He went into the hospital and the blood clot got aloose and entered his brain and paralyzed his left side.

IT wasn't long after his surgery, that I came in to work and was told that all of the funding for the program had been cut and that the program would end. We all broke down and cried as my clients wondered what they were going to do, and how were they going to make it without Mr. Staley. That's the part that hurt me. I had changed their lives and they had certainly changed mine. Even though they were grown, they would get angry when they couldn't perform a task that we can do without any effort. They wanted to learn so bad. I told them that God had brought them this far and he wouldn't leave them. The program closed and they were sent to several other facilities. That was my most satisfying job that I've ever had.

About this time the Lord told me to get chauffeur's license. I tried to argue with him, as I said I'm not going to be driving anything where I'll need chauffeur's license. This time louder and with force He said, get chauffeur's license. I said yes Sir. I went down to take the test and when I saw all of the questions on the test, I told the lady that I would go ahead and take the test and all I missed I would study and come back take the test over. I made 98 on the test. I know that was God. I got my chauffeur's license and a short time later, the pastor bought an older model over the road bus and said, I'm putting you in charge of it. I said I've never driven a bus before and the Lord reminded me of the night at the night club when the white bus driver had me drive his bus.

I began driving the bus for the church, taking other churches across the country. By the time I had gotten the feel of driving the bus, I carried a Christian youth group to Chicago to a convocation for a week. I carried another driver with me and every day we would go to the parking lot where a lot of busses were parked and check on the bus to make sure it would start. It was in the dead of winter. The third day we went to the lot and as we came near the lot, I didn't see our bus. I told the other driver, our bus is gone. Just that morning as we watched the news, two airplanes had been stolen from the air field and we laughed. Other busses sitting there but our bus is gone. I called the pastor and told him what had happened. The police, the insurance company, other pastors searched for the bus but is was never seen again. One of the pastors there knew our pastor and let us borrow one of his busses to bring the group home.

About three months later the insurance settled the claim and the pastor told me to go to the charter bus company where we had the bus serviced and buy another bus. At that time they had about twelve buses for sale. I went down and began to look them over. When I had looked at all of them, the Lord said, 257. That was the number of one of the buses. I went back and looked at all of the buses again and again the Lord said, 257.

I called the pastor and told him I had found the bus. He came down and we test drove the bus and he bought it. I drove the bus. A beautiful coach, from coast to coast. Sometimes as it was breaking day and we were thousands of miles from home and I would look up into the rear view mirror see all 47 souls sleep, I had to ask the Lord, what am I doing out here?

About this time I began to have more dreams and visions that would change my life and reveal my ministry that God had called me for. I will reveal more about it farther into the book.

God was still working miracles. This time the church had gone to Omaha to a church service and I had driven the church's van. I left Kansas City with a full tank of gas. The pastor drove his car with some of the saints. When we arrived, I had a ¼ of a tank left. Church was over about 1 a.m. and I told the pastor that I only had a quarter of a tank of gas. He said, we'll get some and we got on the highway. It was dark and every station we came to was closed and he was getting farther and farther out of sight. Pretty soon the needle went to empty and I'm beginning to draw up because I know if we don't come to a gas station soon we will run out. The pastor is out of sight. Now the needle is past empty and I am really scared. My passengers are talking and don't know what's going on. I'm looking for the engine to cough and then quit running. Finally I saw some bright lights up ahead and something was open. I pulled in and it was a service station and the pastor was there. Talk about someone glad to see a service station, it was me. When I began to look around, I recognized this station. It was by K.C.I Airport. We were only twenty some miles from home. I couldn't believe we had driven all that way on a ¼ of a tank of gas. We had driven about 180 miles on a ¼ of a tank of gas. God has made a true believer of me. That there is nothing He can't do.

One day I was lying across my bed sleep, when the Lord shook me and woke me up. I sat up on the side of the bed and He said look out the window. I looked out and saw my neighbor's car on fire in the garage under his home. Him and the neighbor next door had tried to put it out but is was burning real good. The Lord spoke and said, back your car up to his burning car and attach your chain to the axle and pull it out of his garage. I got up got dressed, ran out of the house, started my car and backed up to his car. Evelyn began screaming and crying don't go in there. My neighbor pleaded with me not to do it that the car was going to explode. He said let it burn. God said do it and I wasn't afraid. I got down as low as I could with the smoke so thick I couldn't hardly see. I crawled to his car and found the axle and hooked my chain around it and crawled out of the smoke and got in my car and began to drag the burning car out from the house. I drug it out into the street and by the time the fire trucks got there the car was burned up.

The only damage done was to the hot water tank and some of the joists in the ceiling were scorched. My neighbor and his wife, who were elderly people couldn't thank me enough but it was God who had instructed me to do it. In about 84, the wife died. Evelyn and I would do different things for them and go to the store for them and even though we were poor and still, we would buy them little gifts. I would never charge them for anything we did for them because I knew they were on fixed income. One week, we had been in Chicago to visit my oldest brother. We had about 500 dollars in bills that we had left at home. My brother told me he had a job to pour a concrete drive and said he would pay me 700 dollars to help him. I knew I would be in the bed a week after the job, but we needed the money. I said I would be glad to help him. The people cancelled the contract and both of us was hurt and sad. I ask the Lord why, when I had all of those bills back home.

We left and came home wondering where the money was coming from. Mr. Brown told Evelyn when she came to clean his house, that he had tried to contact us because he had been sick. This was about 1987. Evelyn had to go to work the next day. I carried her to work and while I was there, our daughter called and said Mr. Brown had called for me. I told her to tell him, I would be right there. I arrived at his house and found him sitting at his kitchen table. I told him to get dressed so I could take him to the hospital. As usual he gave me his house keys, showed me where he had money and his pistol hidden. I found him some clothes to put on and went to bring the car up to this walkway, because he weighed almost 400 pounds. When I returned he still wasn't dressed. He began to tell me what a rough life he had, going from one foster home to the next. How Evelyn and I had stood by him when his wife had gotten sick and died. I called 911 and his next of kin. While we were waiting for the ambulance, he laid back in his armchair and took a deep breath and died.

The ambulance arrived along with a fire truck and it took all of us to get him on the stretcher and into the ambulance. I followed them to the hospital. and was met there by his female cousin. I turned all of his property over to her, consoled her and then I left. The next day she came to our house and said, Mr. Staley you and your wife better take a seat. I thinking to myself, now what is it. She said I found my cousin's safe deposit box and he had something for you both. She went into her purse and pulled out two envelopes and handed them to us. As we opened the envelopes in astonishment, there were two 500 dollar saving bonds with our names on them. He had left instructions to make sure we received them. That was more than enough money to pay our bills. God is truly faithful.

By this time, I'm driving 257 bus full time for the church. I had always wanted to go to Disney Land in California but I knew I wouldn't have enough money so I put that thought out of my mind. A family called and made plans for a trip to California for a week. We made it to California and checked into the motel. The next day I was given the itinerary for the trip. At the top of the list was Disney Land. I had the money, but the park let the bus drivers in free and gave me a free meal. God is just good. The next day was a picnic on the beach. After I got them set up on the beach, and made sure they didn't need me, I took a stroll along the beach by myself. As I walked along the beach with my head down, I had walked quite a distance when I stopped and turned and looked out across the water. There to my shocking surprise was this huge black ship sitting there about 400 feet out in the water. Chills ran down my spine as I thought, this is the same ship I saw in my dream. I wondered, what is going on?

Finally the week was over and we headed home. I dropped the people off where I had picked them up and drove home because I had another trip to make. There was just enough time to dump the pot and clean the bus up. This trip would take me thru the Ozark Mountains to Arkansas. I got the people to their destination and back again. I carried the bus to the bus charter company to have the brakes adjusted and have it greased. The mechanic down in the pit under the bus, said you know your brake booster is missing. I said what? I went down into the pit and looked up at the rear duel wheels and sure enough the brake booster was missing. The rubber air hose that was attached to the booster was wedged between the brake drum and the axle so that the air pressure couldn't escape. The air hose was pinched together and wedged into that space. Somebody's hand had to have done this. It couldn't happen by accident. I don't know where it happened, whether in California or in the Ozarks. I didn't know it was missing because I never lost any air pressure. No one had worked on the bus until I brought it into the shop. The mechanic asked me who had wedged the hose in the space. I said my Father as I stood there with tears in my eyes and my heart about to burst with joy. All I could do was praise Him and give Him the glory. He's worthy to be praised.

I had the bus parked in front of my house and had swept up all the trash and was getting ready to mop the floor. I had the engine running with the air condition on. It started to get hot and I went forward and checked the air gauge and saw there was only about 10 pounds of pressure when there should have been about 180 pounds. I call the shop and talked to the head mechanic and explained the problem. He said, Staley the gear on your air compressor is gone. He said the gear cost about 15.00 and the labor would run about 400 dollars.

When there is no air in the system, all the brakes are locked. To release the brakes I would have to put air in the emergency tank and drive as fast as I could to get to the shop before all the air was gone. I hung up the phone and the Lord spoke and said, Take it out and fix it. I said, I can't do that. This bus cost 65,000 dollars and I have never worked on a bus. Plus I don't have the tools. This time with force He said, Take it out and fix it. I knew He meant what He said. I went to the shop and purchased the gear and purchased a complete ½ inch socket set and returned home to the bus. It was a real hot summer day and Evelyn and the kids had left the house leaving me alone. I opened the rear doors to the engine and I saw the compressor attached to the front of the big Detroit diesel engine. I didn't say it loud, but I had to wonder, Lord what have you gotten me into?

I crawled under the bus to the front of the engine where the transmission was. I could see it real good from this point. To get to it I had to climb on top of the transmission. I had to bend and squeeze myself over the transmission. I got stuck and couldn't go forward and couldn't back out. I was so wedged in I couldn't move. I was all alone. No one knew I was under the bus. It was really hot and I was about to panic. I calmed myself and began to wiggle my way out from over the transmission and out from under the bus. I knew that wasn't it.

On the inside of the bus, in the rear, on the floor right in front of the restroom door was a square foot opening and I removed it. The compressor was right there. The hole was just big enough for my arms to fit in. I began to disconnect the hoses and hot oil began squirting out and I got them all plugged. Finally I got the compressor unbolted and it was bigger than it looked. I was barely able to lift it out of the hole. Sure enough the gear was stripped. I put the new gear on and started to put it back together but after about one or two hours, I couldn't get the teeth on the gear to mesh with the gear on the engine. It was real hot and sweat ran down like rain. As I sat there pondering on what to do next, the Lord began to speak and said, get someone and have them to hit the starter button while you hold the compressor in place. I said Praise the Lord, then I thought I'm here by myself. Who can I get? Just then the voice of a young boy outside said, what are you doing in there? With joy I said, come here you are just the one I'm looking for. He came into the bus grinning and I had him sit in the driver's seat. I told him don't tough anything until I tell you. I said you see this button, when I tell you, press it and let it go. I went to the back of the bus and held the compressor in place.

I said, hit it, and he pressed the button and let it go. The big diesel engine rocked once and almost knocked me over, but nothing happened. I said hit it again and nothing happened. I said hit it again, in the Name of the Father, the Son and the Holy Ghost and the compressor slipped into place. Talk about a happy person I was one happy person.

I bolted the compressor in place and attached all the lines to it, went up front and thanked the little boy. I hit the starter button and it fired right up and the air pressure came up to where it was suppose to be. God not only told me what to do, he also provided the help I needed. God had to teach me that no matter what He told me to do, or how far fetched it seemed, He would bring me thru. I had to learn obedience. Two or three times I told the Lord, no, I wasn't sure of myself because I wasn't sure of Him. The more I began to love Him, the more I began to trust Him. Trust is only faith and faith is born out of love for the Lord.

As Paul said in Philippians 3.13 & 14...Brethren, I count not myself to have apprehended, but this one thing I do, forgetting those things which are behind, and reaching forth unto those things which are before...I press toward the mark for the prize of the calling of God in Christ Jesus. In II Corinthians the twelfth chapter, Paul also said a messenger of satan was sent to buffet him, and he besought the Lord thrice that it might depart from him. The Lord said...Verse 9, My grace is sufficient for thee, for my strength is made perfect in weakness. Then Paul said in verse 10-Therefore I take pleasure in infirmities, in reproaches, in necessities, in persecutions, in distresses for Christ's sake: for when I am weak, then am I strong. I have experienced all of the above both before and after I was converted, but during the 15 years I have been saved, I'm just now getting to the point that I can take pleasure in my many sufferings, knowing that Christ's strength is made perfect in my weakness. Also, knowing that the power of Christ rest upon me in the person of the Holy Ghost.

On one occasion I had bought a gallon of gas and told my daughter to set it down stairs over by the garage door which was in the basement of the house. She sat it down in the utility room by the hot water tank. I think I was reading the Bible in the front room and Evelyn was busy in the kitchen. She came into the front room and said, Honey I smell gas, and I said it's probably coming from next door. There was a plumbing yard next to our lot and when ever they gassed up their vehicles, the gas fumes would come into the house. Evelyn went back to doing what ever she was doing, I continued to read. The Lord said, get up and see. I got up and looked next door and nothing was going on. I wondered, where was the fumes coming from? The Lord said, go down stairs. I went down stairs and opened the door of the utility room and stepped into a puddle of gas. I picked up the dripping gas can and looked to see if the gas was under the hot water tank and it was. As soon as I looked down at the water tank, there was a great explosion and a great fire ball engulfed me and the dripping, half full gas can. It was as if a giant hand picked me up and set me about 15 feet over into the other part of the basement. It set me over there on my feet, gas can still dripping gas. I just knew something had to be missing.

I sat the can down and began to check my clothes and the hair on my head, face and arms. Nothing was missing or even singed. Evelyn heard the explosion and opened the door to the stairs and looked down and saw the fire and went into hysterics, trying to call 911 the police and the fire department. By this time the fire had died down enough for me to squeeze past and she handed me a pot of water and I doused the fire and it was out, with no damage to the house. I had to say, Lord you sent me into that fire.

I hear a lot of people say that God is a way maker, but do they really mean that or it just sound good. I know He's a way maker because I have been there and it is a long way from being over. You're going to have to know that He will make a way because when that day come, and you don't trust Him in the face of death, you will save your life, but loose it. You will turn to every means at your disposal even to denying Christ. You will save your natural life but loose eternal life. Hear what the Spirit is saying.

We need the love that God loves us with, and the only way to love as God has loved us is thru the Holy Spirit because Galatians 5...22 & 23...says...But the fruit of the Spirit is love...Joy is love's strength, peace is love's, security long-suffering is love's patience, gentleness is love's conduct, goodness is love's character, faith is love's confidence, meekness is love's humility, temperance is love's victory: against such there is no such law...A Holy

Spirit controlled person needs no law to cause him or her to live a righteous life. St. John 13...24 & 25, Jesus himself speaking said, a new commandment I give unto you, that ye love one another, as I have love you, that ye also love one another. By this shall all men know that ye are my disciples, if ye have love one to another. I pray to the Holy Spirit, take over my life completely that I may love as Christ has commanded.

I had a trip to Omaha, and the money I was paid, I left it with Evelyn. We were to spend the night in Omaha. I would have to sleep on the bus. About forty miles from the city, the Lord said, testify. I picked up the mike to the intercom and began to testify. of how the Lord had saved me and how He had saved my life so many times. The people woke up, the pastor woke and came to the front of the bus. The people began to shout and praise the Lord and we had church on the bus. When I finished, I put the mike up and the people began to take their seats. The pastor said, we've had church and we want to take up a love token for Bro. Staley. While they were taking up the offering, the praises and tears began to flow and I could not help myself. I began to feel love flowing from deep with in me. I knew a few of the people and the pastor, but most of the people I didn't know. The love kept getting stronger and stronger. It got so strong that I had to pull the bus over and hug and show my love to everyone on the bus. As I started to pull the bus over, the over flowing love left and I was able to go on into Omaha. I wondered what was going on.

I have come across people who love only those in their own church, those in their financial or social status and even those of only their race. Christ is not pleased with this.

We finally made it into Omaha and went to the motel and when I counted the money, it was twice what the motel would cost me. God is my very life. I remember when I got saved, Evelyn and the kids had gone away and I was home alone. It was a beautiful sunny day and the windows and front door were open and breeze was blowing thru the windows. I was rejoicing and praising God walking thru the house. I thought I was talking to myself and I asked the question, Lord am I really saved, am I walking with you and are you really walking with me. I had forgotten all about it, and about twenty or thirty minutes later I began to feel like I was naked to the point, that even though I was fully clothed, I had to look at myself to make sure I was clothed. I began to feel like the roof was about to fall in on me. I began to feel like I was the only person in the world. Even though the sun was shinning brightly, I felt like it was midnight. Stark fear came upon me and as I was about to run screaming from the house, just as suddenly as it had come upon me, it left me.

I stood there wondering what had happened. The Lord asked me, remember what you asked me, if I was walking with you. My mind went back and I said yes. The Lord had taken His spirit from me to let me know how it feel without His presence. I said Lord I remember and I will never ask that again. I use to wonder why did all these things happen to me and why had God revealed all these things to me. Even though I benefited from the revelations and the experiences, they were for you. They are a witness to you, so you can know the love and power of God that you may know that God is faithful and that you may know what is coming upon this nation.

One of the churches that we belonged to was when the pastor wasn't speaking his elite group wouldn't speak either. This was one of those occasions and one of the missionaries that hadn't been speaking, broke her silence and said, Bro. Staley may I speak to you for a minute and I said sure. She said Bro. Staley last night I had a dream and I saw you and Sister Staley on a wall looking down on us. She said the Lord told me you were the watchman on the wall. She was frightened as she told me this. In my spirit I knew she was right, but I guess I hadn't come to that point.

All of the dreams or visions that I had, prior to the following dreams, have come to pass exactly the way the Lord showed it to me, and just as those had come to pass, I know these will come to pass as well and God wants you to know this.

The Lord began to lead me into the scriptures and what He began to reveal to me, I wasn't quite ready for. I went to Numbers 12-6...And He said, hear now my words, if there be a prophet among you, I the Lord will make myself known unto him in a vision, and will speak unto him in a dream... I didn't want to read anymore. That is exactly what the Lord had done and I wanted to deny that the Lord was speaking to me. I knew of a few men that I thought were great enough for God to give this to them...Finally I said, not my will, but let Your will be done.

Amos 3-7...Surely the Lord God will do nothing, but He revealeth His secret unto His servants the prophets...

Habakkuk 2-2 & 3...And the Lord answered me, and said, write the vision, and make it plain upon tables, that he may run that readeth it...for the vision is yet for an appointed time, but at the end it shall speak, and not lie, though it tarry, wait for it: because it will surely come, it will not tarry...

Ezekiel 33: 1 thru 9...Again the word of the Lord came unto me, saying son of man speak to the children of thy people, and say unto them, when I bring the sword upon a land, if the people of the land take a man of their coasts, and set him for their watchman: ...if when he seeth the sword come upon the land, he blow the trumpet, and warn the people...Then whosoever heareth the sound of the trumpet, and taketh not warning, if the sword come, and taketh him away, his blood shall be upon his own head...He heard the sound of the trumpet, and took not warning, his blood shall be upon him. But he that taketh warning shall deliver his soul...But if the watchman see the sword come, and blow not the trumpet, and the people be not warned: if the sword come, and take any person from among them, he is taken away in his iniquity, but his blood will I require at the watchman's hand...So thou o son of man I have set thee a watchman unto the house of Israel, therefore when I say unto the wicked, O wicked man, thou shalt surely die: if thou dost not speak to warn the wicked from his way, that wicked man shall die in his iniquity: but his blood will I require at thine hand...

Nevertheless, if thou warn the wicked of his way to turn from it, if he do not turn from his way, he shall die in his iniquity, but thou hast delivered thou soul...

The Lord showed me something that at first I didn't understand, but after I began to think on it, tears began to stream down my face...The Lord showed me a huge umbrella open, and the sky was a pretty blue and the sun was shinning brightly. People of all races were dancing and playing and doing what ever they wanted to do. Soon a small dark cloud appeared and began to get bigger and bigger. Then the cloud covered the sun and it got dark. It began to storm and rain. The lightening flashed and all the people ran under the umbrella and it protected them all.

Soon the storm stopped, the clouds began to dissipate and the sun began to shine.

As soon as all the black clouds had rolled away and the sun was shinning, all the people ran back out into the sunshine. What the Lord was letting me know, is He is that umbrella of protection and when the storms of life come upon us, we run to God for protection and He protects us. But as soon as everything is alright, we go back to doing whatever it was we were doing before the storm. We leave God. I wept as I thought about, here is God, the Creator of this universe letting me know how He felt about how His people were doing Him. I felt His sadness as the tears ran down my face and I told Him, Lord I will never leave you.

Isaiah 58.1...Cry loud, spare not, lift up thy voice like a trumpet, and shew my people their transgression, and the house of Jacob their sins.

Jeremiah 6.17...Also I set watchmen over you, saying, hearken to the sound of the trumpet...but they said, we will not hearken...

Jeremiah 7.1 thru 15...The word that came to Jeremiah from the Lord saying, ...Stand in the gate of the Lord's house, and proclaim there this word, and say, hear the word of the Lord, all ye of Juda, that enter in at these gates to worship the Lord...Thus saith the Lord of Host, the God of Israel, amend your ways and your doings, and I will cause you to dwell in this place...

Trust ye not in lying words, saying the temple of the Lord, the temple of the Lord, the temple of the Lord, are these...

For if you thoroughly amend your ways and your doings: if ye thoroughly execute judgment between a man and his neighbor: ...If ye oppress not the stranger, the fatherless, and the widow, and shed not innocent blood in this place, neither walk after other gods to your hurt; ...then will I cause you to dwell in this place, in the land that I gave to your fathers, for ever and ever...Behold ye trust in lying words, that can not profit...will you steal, murder, and commit adultery, and swear falsely, and burn incense unto Baal, and walk after other gods whom ye know not? ...and come and stand before me in this, house, which is called by my name, and say, we are delivered to do all these abominations. Is this house, which is called by my name, become a den of robbers in your eyes? Behold, even I have seen it, saith the Lord...But go ye now unto my place which was in Shiloh, where I set my name at the first, and see what I did to it for the wickedness of my people Israel...and now, because ye have done all these works, saith the Lord, and I speak unto you, rising up early and speaking, but ye heard not: and I called you, but ye answered not...therefore will I do unto this house, which is called by my name, wherein ye trust, and unto the place which I gave to you and to your fathers, as I have done to Shiloh...and I will cast you out of my sight, as I have cast out all your brethren, even the whole seed of Ephraim.

Jeremiah 8.5 thru 13...Why then is this people of Jerusalem slidden back by a perpetual backsliding? They hold fast deceit, they refuse to return...I harkened and heard, but they spake not aright: no man repented him of his wickedness, saying, what have I done? Everyone turned to his course, as the horse rusheth into the battle...Yea the stork in the heaven knoweth her appointed times: and the turtle and the crane and the swallow observe the time of their coming: but my people know not the judgment of the Lord...How do we say, we are wise, and the law of the Lord is with us? Lo, certainly in vain made he it: the pen of the scribes is in vain...The wise men are ashamed, they are dismayed and taken: Lo, they have rejected the word of the Lord, and what wisdom is in them? Therefore will I give unto others, and their fields to them that shall inherit them: for everyone from the least even unto the greatest is given to covetousness. From the prophet even unto the priest, everyone dealeth falsely...for they have healed the hurt of the daughter of my people slightly, saying peace, peace, when there is no peace...were they ashamed when they had committed abominations? Nay, they were not at all ashamed, neither could they blush: therefore shall they fall among them that fall: in the time of their visitation, they shall be cast down, saith the Lord: ...I will surely consume them, saith the Lord: there shall be no grapes on the vine, nor figs on the fig tree, and the leaf shall fade: and the things that I have given them shall pass away from them.

Joel 2.1 & 2...and 11 thru 17...Blow ye the trumpet in Zion, and sound an alarm in my holy mountain: let all the inhabitants of the land tremble: for the day of the Lord cometh, for it is nigh at hand...A day of darkness and of gloominess, a day of clouds and thick darkness, as the morning spread upon the mountains: ...and the Lord shall utter His voice before His army: for His camp is very great: for He is strong that executeth His word: for the day of the Lord is great and very terrible: and who can abide it? ...Therefore also now, saith the Lord, turn ye even to me with all your heart, and with fasting, and with weeping, and with mourning: ...and rend your heart, and not your garments and turn unto the Lord your God: for he is gracious and merciful, slow to anger, and of great kindness, and repenteth him of the evil...Verse 15...Blow the trumpet in Zion, sanctify a fast, call a solemn assembly...Gather the people, sanctify the congregation, assemble the elders, gather the children, and those that suck the breast: let the bridegroom go forth of his chamber and the bride out of her closet...Let the priests, the ministers of the Lord weep between the porch and the alter, and let them say, spare thy people, O Lord, and give not thine heritage to reproach, that the heathen should rule over them: wherefore should they say among the people, where is their god?

Romans 5.12...Wherefore, as by one man sin entered into the world, and death by sin: and so death passed upon all men, for that, all have sinned. (That man was Adam).

Romans 5.17 to 19...For if by one man's offense death reigned by one: much more they which receive abundance of grace and of the gift of righteousness shall reign in by one...Jesus Christ)...Therefore by the offense of one, judgment came upon all men to condemnation: even so by the righteousness of one the free gift came upon all men unto justification of life...For as by one man's disobedience many were made sinners, so by the obedience of one shall many be made righteous...

Please hear what the Holy Spirit is saying...to escape the judgment that's coming upon this nation, you have to come to Christ, and let Him wash you of your sins.

Acts 4.10 to 12...Be it known unto you all, and to all the people of Israel, that by the Name of Jesus Christ of Nazareth, whom ye crucified, whom God raised from the dead, even by Him doth this man stand here before you whole...This is the stone which was set at naught of you builders, which is become the head of the corner...neither is there salvation in any other: for there is none other name under heaven given among men, whereby we must be saved.

Galatians 5. 19-21... Now the works of the flesh are manifest, which are these: <u>adultery</u>... wherein a man, married or single, has illicit sex with a married or betrothed woman... fornication... crime of impurity between unmarried persons... uncleaness... homosexuality... lasciviousness... shameful conduct, idolatry... an object of worship other than God... witchcraft... the occult, working of spells, fortune telling... hatred... dislike, enmity... variance... differences that produces controversy, discord, division... emulations... attempting to equal, surpass or out do another... wrath... violent anger, rage, fury... strife... conflict, struggle with... seditions... act of disturbing the peace... heresies... opinions contrary to orthodox teaching, faith, or belief... envyings... to grudge another person's good fortune, success, jealousy... murders... to kill with premeditated intent, drunkenness... excessive drinking... revellings... entertainment with music, dancing, noisy celebration... and such like: of which I tell you before as I have told you in time past, that they which do such things shall not inherit the Kingdom of God.

GOD'S JUDGMENT OF AMERICA

Amos 3-7—says,—surely the Lord God will do nothing, but He revealeth His secret unto His servants the prophets...

Isaiah 58-1—says—Cry loud, spare not, lift up thy voice like a trumpet, and shew my people their transgression, and the house of Jacob their sins...

I am lifting up my voice like a trumpet to warn who ever will listen, about God's coming judgments upon America.

The Lord showed me a vision of His church, and how He see the end time church. As I entered the front door of the church, a man met me at the door, and asked me if I was ready to go to the sanctuary. I said yes. As we stood there, I noticed how beautiful the church was. There was gold curtains and tapestries and beautiful gold trimmed furniture, huge golden chandeliers with thick red carpet on the floor.

As we turned to go up the stairs to the sanctuary, people began to come into the church for service. They were people of all races. As I looked at them coming in the women were wearing long and short dresses with splits up the front, sides and back. Most of the dresses were low cut in the front, exposing their bosom. Long dangling ear rings and high heeled shoes. Many had their hair dyed different colors.

The men were dressed in tuxedos and had on highly polished shoes, with a small corsage on their lapels. I looked at these people of all races coming into God's house. The man and I continued up the stairs to the second floor. As we arrived on the second floor, I could hear that there was church going on. The floor was divided into four rooms, and as I looked into the first room they were having church.

As I looked closer, I saw all white people. I looked in the next room and there were all black people. I looked in the next room and there were all oriental.

I looked into the last room, and they were all red people. Men and women of all races came through the front doors together, but once inside, they segregated themselves. Sunday morning, one of the most holy days in American, is one of the most segregated days in America. Churches are not only segregated by race and ethnic culture, but by doctrines, denominations, social and financial standards.

Ephesians 4.1 thru 6...says, I therefore, the prisoner of the Lord, beseech you that ye walk worthy of the vocation wherewith ye are called...with all lowliness and meekness, with long-suffering, forbearing one another in love, endeavoring to keep the unity of the spirit in the bond of peace. There is one body, and one Spirit, even as ye are called in one hope of your calling, One Lord, One Faith, One Baptism, One God and Father of all, who is above all, and through all, and in you all.

When Jesus Christ died on the cross, the curtain separating the Holy of Holies from the rest of the temple, was rent in twain, giving man, through Jesus Christ, free access into the very presence of God. Man has built the partitions back into the church.

We went up to the next floor, and once again the floor was divided into four rooms. As I looked into each room, there were choirs singing but they were segregated and singing different songs. Churches, choirs, and singers are taking words and music from the world, and bringing it into a holy church and call themselves singing to a Holy God. He has said in His word, be ye holy, for I am holy.

We went to the next floor and it was also divided. I looked into the first room and there were every kind of percussion instrument that is made. Beautiful drums of all shapes, sizes and colors. The instruments were so beautiful, that I made a mental notation that after I finished the service, I would return and look at the instruments.

I looked in the next room and saw the most beautiful pianos and organs of all shapes and colors. I was amazed at the beauty of all that I was looking at. I looked in the next room, and there were beautiful wind instruments. There were all kinds and sizes of brass horns, trumpets, saxophones of different colors.

I looked into the last room and there were every kind of stringed instrument that is made.

All of the floors were covered with beautiful thick red carpet, but when we arrived at the top floor where the sanctuary was, the floor was beautiful marble. To my amazement, there were hospital beds around the sanctuary door. As I started toward the door, there were people in the beds, and they raised up and looked at me as if they had no hope at all.

In my mind, I asked the Lord, why are these people in beds around the sanctuary? He turned my attention to the people of all races coming into the church for service. The way they were dressed represents pride and vain glory. The church has segregated herself from herself. The church is not only allowing some of everything to go on in the church, but coming to be entertained. People are attending church because it's being a good citizen, and not to hear from God. They are coming to hear the music and the choirs sing...because these conditions exist in the church, the people are spiritually sick, spiritual sickness, bring physical sickness.

Jeremiah 6.16...says, Thus saith the Lord, stand ye in the ways, and see, and ask for the old paths, where is the good way, and walk there in, and ye shall find rest for your souls. But they said, we will not walk there in.

II Chronicles 7.13 & 14...says, If I shut up heaven that there be no rain, or if I command the locusts to devour the land, or if I send pestilence among my people; if my people which are called by my name, shall humble themselves, and pray, and seek my face, and turn from their wicked ways, then will I hear from heaven, and will forgive their sin, and will heal their land.

The Lord showed me in a dream, buildings all across this nation with closed signs, on the front of the buildings. Then he showed me shops and stores open and doing business. But the people doing business were Asian people. There is not many items or merchandise on the market today that does not say, Made in China, Made in Japan, Made in Taiwan, Made in Korea, or made in some other Asian country. As this country is flooded with the imports of these countries, many companies across this nation has had to close and go out of business.

Many more companies are moving out of this nation to foreign countries because of cheap labor and greed. How long can a nation last with this type of greed, not only in commerce, but in all facets of our nation.

As I watched our former president, on national television, try to defend himself in the sex scandal when he was exposed, I wept not only for him but for this nation. Those that were exposing him and pulling out all of his dirty laundry, was in effect exposing the shameful immorality of this nation. I saw this great nation in the spot light. Jeremiah 18.7 & 8...says, At what instant I shall speak concerning a nation, and concerning a kingdom, to pluck up, and to pull down, and to destroy it: if that nation, against whom I have pronounced, turn from their evil, I will repent of the evil that I thought to do unto them. In this book, God is speaking to this nation.

GOD'S JUDGMENT OF AMERICA

God showed in a dream, me walking around down town on a beautiful sunny day. The skies were a beautiful blue. It could have been any city in America. I was looking at all the people going in and coming out of the stores shopping. People were sitting in restaurants eating and talking. People were everywhere enjoying the beautifully day.

All of a sudden, fire began to fall from heaven. I don't know if it was a nuclear attack from another country, of if it was fire from heaven. Fire was falling all around me but none was falling on me. People by the thousands were running and trying to get away from the fire and destruction. Buildings were crumbling like toy houses. Skyscrapers were crumbling to the ground. Thousands upon thousands of bodies of people of all races were everywhere. The ground trembled so, people trying to walk acted as if they were drunk. Molten concrete mingled with blood ran down the streets like water. Cars and trucks were running into each other and were causing traffic jams as the people tried to escape from the city and the destruction. I looked to my right and saw a woman that had fallen. She looked me in my eyes with stark fear, lifted her arm up to me and said, Mister please help me. I reached down and grabbed her hand, at the same time a piece of building fell and crushed her to death, leaving me holding her arm. A woman on my left had fallen also and looked at me with fear in her eyes and asked for my help. As I reached down to help her, the same thing happened to her. In the midst of all the screaming and crying, I had to stand there watch the death and destruction. God was showing me what is about to take place in America, and

I'm trying to warn you. What you do about this revelation from God is left up to you.

The Lord showed me, my family without faces and my self in a house. The house we were in was moving over the debris and bodies from the destruction. When the house came to a stop, I looked out of the window and saw that we were out in the desert, away from the destruction. I could still see the fire from the city burning and hear the terrible screaming and crying. The Lord had saved me and my family. I asked the Lord the meaning of this dream, because I know a house can't move off of it's foundation.

In 1985, about two or three years after the dream, my father, who was getting up in age, had been living on his own. Because of his senility, he didn't get along with people. One day as I stopped by his senior citizen apartment, I found out that he had gotten into a fight with another senior citizen. He had to move. He didn't want to move with me, so I told him that I would renovate my whole basement for him to move in. He didn't want that. I found another senior apartment for him and moved him into it. After a very short stay, there was another altercation in which he had to move. Because I've had three operations on my lower spine and one operation in my neck and chest for my spine, the first move was hard. I had to discord box upon box full of rusty can goods that he had been storing. Piles and piles of clothing and now I was going to have to move him again. Unable to work, I didn't have the money to have someone move him, so my wife and I were prepared to move him again.

He didn't want to move to another senior apartment and he didn't want to move with me. I loved my father, but I had to ask my God, why had this burden been placed on me.

We sat down and began to discuss different options. We talked about putting a mobile-home or travel trailer in my backyard and he liked the idea. I checked with the city ordinance, and it wasn't allowed. We then thought a motor home would fit the bill. My father, wife and myself were all excited about a motor home. I had no idea of what they cost and hadn't thought about the money part of it. My dad had me to take him to his bank and to my shocking surprise withdrew twenty one thousand dollars. My dad being tight when it came to money of four or five dollars has withdrawn this money and got me carrying it in my waistband of my pants. This is happening so fact it is like I'm in a dream.

On the way to taking my dad back to his apartment, I come back to reality. I began to think, Lord I don't want to covetous or greedy over this money or motor home. I said Dad, I'm going to put this money back into the bank and think of something else. My dad said, E.L. keep that money and that we were going to find something we wanted. What ever belonged to my dad, was his but now he has put me in his equation. This was his, to be bought with his money, for him to live in, but he is saying we. I'm saying to myself, what is going on here? We found a nice 29 ft. Pace Arrow Motor home. He asked me, do you like it? I asked him, do you like it? We are asking each other the same question over and over. My wife fell in love with the motor home.

My dad looked at me and said, if you like it, get it. We paid eighteen thousand five hundred dollars for the motor home.

I put the motor home in my back yard and plugged the power cord into my house and my dad was very happy and satisfied. We would take trips from time to time and I would keep the holding tanks dumped and keep his propane tank full. I made sure he was comfortable.

I think it was about the beginning of the third year of my father living in the motor home, that Evelyn and I were in the motor home talking with my dad. We were asking him about God and Jesus and about hell. He said he didn't want to go to hell. We had prayer with him according to Romans 10.9 & 10...and my father received the Lord as his Savior that day.

Whenever we prepared our dinner, we would take my father a plate of food. Right after he received the Lord as his Savior, I noticed he had stopped eating. I began to inquire as to what was wrong with him, and he would reply, nothing. He was always a slim figure of a man, but now I've noticed that he is getting even thinner. I began to cry and he asked me what was wrong, and I told him I was worried about him. He told me that he wasn't sick, he just wasn't hungry and not for me to worry about him. He had made his peace with God. I called his doctor, human services, and the police and told them my dad was not eating and that I was worried about his health. They told me there was nothing they are I could do. My father went about 15 or 20 days without food and very little water and in my presence, the Lord called him home.

When we filled out the papers for the motor home, we both signed the title as co-owners. Now I was the owner of the motor home and this was the house that the Lord had shown me in the dream.

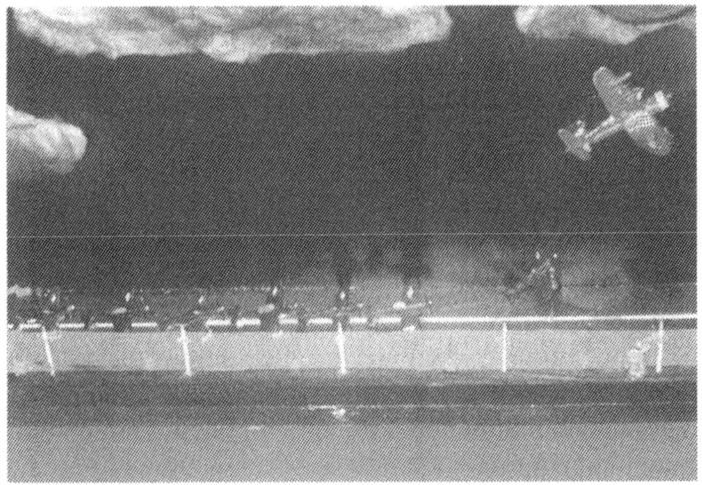

The Lord showed me standing at a high wire fence, looking through it to see a line of airplanes as far as I could see. I was standing in total darkness looking at the planes, when the first plane started it's engine. Seems like it was warming up the engine or waiting for the order to take off. Then it began to taxi down the runway in slow motion and slowly it began to climb into the air. I am standing there in the dark looking at this plane about twenty feet above my head, when suddenly I heard a sound of a huge cannon, boom.

Suddenly a bright light shown down from heaven and spot lighted the plane. In slow motion, the plane rolled over exposing it's under carriage. The spot light illuminated the American Flag painted on it's belly. The plane, after showing me the American flag, slowly fell to the ground without being destroyed. A piece of machinery moved onto the runway and moved the plane to the side of the runway.

As soon as this was completed, the next plane started up it's engine and began to taxi down the runway to take off. The same thing happened to it. I had to stand there and watch as all of the planes that were lined up on the runway try to take off. Everyone of them were hit with the canon, and everyone rolled over to show me the American flag. God was letting me know that He was judging America. America has the most sophisticated military weapons in the world, but to an all powerful God, they are nothing. It is God that brings the victory. America needs to stop trusting in her military might, and turn back to God. This nation was great because it loved and feared God. God blessed it and put the fear of it in the hearts and minds of other nations. We have lost our fear of God, and the nations have lost their fear of us.

The Lord carried me, in a dream, into a make-shift hospital in a cave under ground. As I walked into the cave, there were beds and cots set up everywhere that there was space. I could hear the screaming and moaning and groaning of those in sever pain and agony. There was blood everywhere. The attending nurses and doctors were covered with blood as they tried to comfort the injured and dying. People of all races suffering and dying. Some were missing arms and legs, others had crushed bodies, while others had sever burns. Those that had died, by the hundreds, were being carried outside and covered. Hundreds were laying outside waiting to be carried inside for treatment. Hundreds were dying while waiting for treatment.

The Lord walked me through this make shift hospital to show me the physical suffering and death that is about to take place in this nation.

May God have mercy on us. This can only give you a glimpse of the destruction and the suffering that's about to take place.

In a dream, the Lord carried me into a grocery store. As I walked around inside of the store, there was blood everywhere. There were no food freezers or coolers as we see in the stores today. There were flies everywhere. In our stores today the food is literally stacked to the ceiling. In this store there were no isles of cereals, canned goods, bread of all kinds, cookies, ice cream, soft drinks, dairy products or candies of all sorts. There were not vegetables and no fruits.

What I saw was table after table with every crawling or creeping creature that could be caught or killed. Some of them were skinned and some of them still had the fur or hair or feathers on them. People of all races were standing in line to buy what they could. You could only buy a little piece of the meat. There is a famine coming upon this land.

Isaiah 13.6 thru 9.11...says, "howl ye, for the day of the Lord is at hand; it shall come as a destruction from the almighty. Therefore shall all hands be faint, and every man's heart shall melt, and they shall be afraid; pangs and sorrows shall take hold of them; they shall be in pain as a woman that travaileth, they shall be amazed one at another; their faces shall be as flames.

Behold, the day of the Lord cometh, cruel both with wrath and fierce anger, to lay the land desolate; and he shall destroy the sinners thereof out of it. And I will punish the world for their evil, and the wicked for their iniquity, and I will cause the arrogancy of the proud to cease, and will lay low the haughtiness of the terrible.

The Lord showed me in a dream, thousands upon thousands of people of all races converging or gathering at a refuse dump. As I walked through the dump and watched the garbage trucks back up to the edge of the huge mound of garbage and dump their load, I could see the people rummaging through the garbage.

They were looking for food to feed their children and families. They were looking for clothing to cloth their families. They were looking for furniture and utensils and anything else they could use in their home.

This is the land of plenty and the land of opportunity, but because we have turned our back on God, the land of plenty will become the land of desolation.

II Chronicles 7.14...says, If my people, which are called by my name, shall humble themselves, and pray, and seek my face, and turn from their wicked ways, then will I hear from heaven, and will forgive their sin, and will heal their land.

In a dream, the Lord placed me in a prison camp, There was a tall wire fence topped with barbed wire on the top and it surrounded the prison camp. I walked around the camp and saw thousands upon thousands of people of all races, sitting or walking round or lying on the ground. They looked as if they had no hope at all.

After I had looked at all the people of all races, the Lord directed my attention to the captors. All of them were Asian soldiers and they were armed with automatic weapons. Some were stationed at different points with machine guns.

Then the Lord pointed out something else to me. It was their military caps. Some wore their military caps with the visor turned up and on their visors I could see a red star as their insignia. The red star was what the Lord pointed out to me.

I was standing by the fence, about four feet from one of the guards who had an automatic weapon. He looked at me and turned his back to me. I kneeled down and began to dig a hole under the fence. When the hole was just big enough for me to squeeze through, I laid down on my back and began to slide under the fence. When my body was half way out, the guard turned around and looked me in my eyes. I froze in position, and to myself, Lord I'm dead. I know this guard is going to kill me because he has caught me trying to escape. As he looked at me for about a second, he, to my surprise, raise his weapon in the air and turned his back to me, and never turned back around. I eased out from under the fence, dusted myself off and quietly walked down the road out of sight of the other guards...Praise be to my God.

I know these visions are coming to pass or I wouldn't be writing this book. I don't know if I will go into captivity or the Lord was just showing me the captivity. I have got to be prepared. I know many of God's prophets went into captivity with their nation, Israel.

One night the Lord shook me and woke me up from sleep. I sat up in bed, in the dark, with my heart pounding, wondering what's going on here. The Lord spoke and said...Feed the people...feed the people...feed the people...He said it three times and each time He said it, He spoke it louder and louder and louder.

As I sat there in total darkness, I thought in my mind, Lord I'm unable to work because of the surgery on my spine, and I'm barely able to feed my family. At that moment the Lord put me back to sleep. In a dream, a man came to my front door and when I answered the door, he said I'm ready to work. I must have known the man or angel, because I said alright. He went around my house to the huge back yard and then he came back to my front door and said, I'm finished. I said alright, let me see what you have done. We went through the house to the back door. He and I stepped out of the door and that is as far as we could go. He had covered the whole back yard with food. There was a mountain of food about three stories high of fresh vegetables, fruit, bread, all kinds of fresh meat, milk and all sorts of good things to eat. I was dumbfounded at that much food and in my back yard.

Stuttering, I asked him, where did he get all the food and how did he stack it so high? What am I going to do with all this food? He began backing up smiling. About that time, people of all races began coming toward my house and the man disappeared into the crowd...God was letting me know, son don't worry about where the food will come from. When the time come, I will supply the food and I want you to feed the people...Even though there is a famine coming upon the land, God is going to provide for His people. You've got to be one of his.

If you are reading this book and you do not know Jesus in the pardon of your sins, get down on your knees now and tell him, I know I am a sinner and deserve to go to hell. Forgive my sins and come into my heart and save me. I know you died for me, and I will live for you.

Romans 5.12...says...Wherefore, as by one man sin entered into the world, and death by sin; and so death passed upon all men, for that all have sinned. This is referring to our forefather, Adam, when Adam sinned in the Garden of Eden, sin entered into the world upon mankind...Romans 5.8 & 9...says...But God commendeth His love toward us, in that, while we were yet sinners, Christ died for us...much more then, being now justified by His blood, we shall be saved from wrath through Him. Christ bled and died on the cross that all who come to Him for forgiveness, shall be justified.

Romans 10.9 & 10...That if thou shalt confess with thy mouth the Lord Jesus, and shall believe in thine heart that God hath raised Him from the dead, thou shalt be saved...for with the heart man believeth unto righteousness; and with the mouth confession is made unto salvation.

In 1993, the Lord impressed upon my heart to sell our house of 25 years and all of our possessions and hit the highway. He didn't tell me where we were going. After we had traveled a bit showing the display of, God's Judgment of America, we ended up in Oklahoma City. We stopped to visit one of my sons, Leslie, and his wife Linda, persuaded us to stay and enroll or granddaughter in grade school. We were living in the motor home in their driveway. What little money we had was getting low and I told my wife, Evelyn that God had allowed me to be taken off of my job as a heavy-equipment operator because of back surgery. I told her that if God wanted me to have a job, he would send it to our door.

The next day there was a knock on the door of the motor home and I said come in. It was a friend of my son, whom I had only met twice. He said, I got a little job you can have if you want it. I looked at my wife as she was smiling from ear to ear. God gave me the grace and the strength to work there 10 months. I started washing pots and pans after the food had been prepared to be taken to senior citizen centers. Sometimes I would drive one of the delivery trucks when one of the drivers were off. Eddie was the head chef and wanted me to help cook the main coarse or the meat coarse of the meal. They cooked in gas and electric pots so big, that I could get in it to clean it. We cooked for no less than 900 people and no more than 1500 people everyday. I got familiar with the equipment and came in one morning and started having more sever pain in my lower back and neck more than usual to the point where I barely could walk. I had to leave the job. I guess I had gotten the experience with the equipment that the Lord wanted me to have.

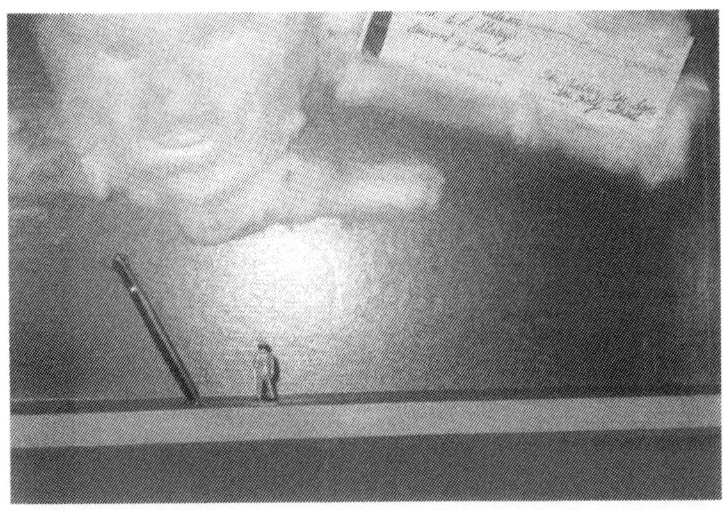

In a vision, the Lord showed me looking up into a beautiful blue sky and there I saw a huge check made out to me. It was made out for one million dollars. Next to the check was a huge white billowy cloud with the face of a man in it with huge eyes as flames of fire. I said father, is this enough to do what you have laid on my heart? The Lord has told me to feed the people. There has to be a facility not only to feed people but to store the food. The Lord has laid it on my heart to build a camp for church and a facility for seniors, widows and fatherless. A place where youth can come and have clean fun while learning about their creator. There will be television and acting out the scriptures in full Biblical dress.

The Lord stuck a huge pen down through the clouds and told me to change the one. I took the pen and blotted out the one. As I wrote in the new number, he blotted the number out of my mind and blocked the number so I couldn't see what number I wrote down. I certainly didn't understand that. Why would God tell me to change the number and then not let me see it?

I was telling an evangelist that I knew about the dream and she ask me if I knew what it meant, and I said no. She said, Brother Staley, that mean there is an unlimited amount of money for the ministry. I was truly excited about what was revealed to me but what really got me excited was God, the Creator of this world looking down at me and talking with me the dust of the ground. That's exciting.

St. Matthew 24.13...says...But he that shall endure unto the end, the same shall be saved...I saw in a vision, a long line of people of all races. The line was as far as I could see. it was a beautiful sunny day and we were marching out through a desert. People had their possessions on their backs, in wagons, some on donkeys and we were rejoicing and singing Zion songs to the Lord. The children were laughing and playing along the way. High praises went up to the God of our salvation...Praise His Holy Name.

There is two dreams that I had along with the other dreams that have not come to pass. These dreams came to pass just as the Lord showed them to me except those two. One shows an airplane that has crashed into a building where mostly women worked at assembly tables. I think the pilot ejected before the crash because I saw him walking through the building in an orange jump suit surveying the damage.

The other one showed an air force jet that crashed into a shallow creek near a over pass or bridge. The pilot was injured but a telephone lineman on a telephone pole rescued him and got him some help. Much of this I don't understand.

In a dream, I saw Jesus sitting on a beautiful throne up in the beautiful blue sky. In the midst of snow white billowy clouds, His face was shinning brighter than the noon day sun. As I stood there gazing up at my Lord, I was completely dumbfounded at His stature and magnificence. He looked like He was four or five hundred feet tall. I felt as though I was nothing. He was sitting there with a scepter in His hand, with His left side facing me. As I looked at Him in awe, He stood up and turned and faced me. I could hardly look for the brightness of His face. I woke up with joy bells ringing in my soul. I had seen the King of Glory. My heart was pounding with excitement. I had to tell somebody. I was so excited, I could hardly get dressed for Sunday School. I saw the vision early Sunday morning.

When my family and I arrived at church, people were going in different directions to their classes. There was an elderly brother, whom the Lord has now called home, who was known as Brother Odem. I would get to church early to unlock the doors and in the winter, make sure the heat was on. Many times he would be sitting on the steps waiting to get in. He didn't have a car. The people would mistreat him, by making excuses when he needed a ride home. But when they were selling tickets or food, he would try to accommodate them all. When they all had turned him down for a ride, I would tell him, come on, I'll take you home.

That morning he was waiting for me. He pulled me over to the side and said, Brother Staley, can I tell you what the Lord showed me last night? I said sure. He said Brother Staley, Last night I saw a man and his face was shinning like the sun. I said you did. He said he looked like he was four or five hundred feet tall. I said he did, getting more excited. He said Brother Staley that man came down to earth. With tears in my eyes I said Brother I saw that same man when he stood up from his throne. Jesus is soon to return. Repent ye and believe the gospel.

The Lord let me know the ministry will include people of all races and that I would have to leave the traditions of men. The Lord has commanded me to feed the people. I'll need facilities and equipment to do this. I want land to build a facility to house the elderly mothers and widows. I will have a facility to bring young people from the streets and other places and show them how to have clean fun, such as a skating rink, go cart track, something for the boys and something for the girls, and for all ages. While teaching them to respect each other as well as themselves, teaching young girls how to be young ladies, and boys how to be young gentlemen. A place for ministers, pastors, missionaries, evangelists, deacons to come and learn to love and respect one another, pray together and really get in touch with God. How to be humble instead of being lifted up in pride. Saints of all races.

A little after I got saved, the Lord told me, as I was on my way home, and at the entrance to the American Cable Vision facility, He said American Cable Vision. Well this is the first time that He has said anything about the cable company and I didn't know why He wanted me to go in. As I past the entrance, I said, well I've past it now, I'll go in the next time I'm down here. I'm not planning to be nowhere close to this place for another month. Maybe God will have told me why He wants me to go there...I just love Him because he still loves us when we think we are out smarting Him. The very next day I'm on my way somewhere and it seem as if I'm in a trance. I don't know where I was going or where I had been. When I came to my self, I was right back at the entrance of the cable company. I wondered how did I get here and the very next day. I turned into the drive and parked, then went inside.

I found the administrator and told him I needed to speak with him. He led me to his office and I began to tell him of the things that the Lord had laid on my heart. I told him I needed to know how to produce a TV program. I know TV will be part of the ministry. When I had finished telling him what I had to say, He just sat there and looked at me. At that point I felt foolish and asked myself, what am I doing here. I'm reminded of what Paul said in I Corinthians 4.10...We are fools for Christ's sake. When we began to walk with Christ, He will call us to do things that are foolish to the world, so not many want to look foolish for Christ. I will look and act foolish, as the world sees me, for His name sake.

After he sat there and looked at me awhile, and I'm wondering what's he thinking about, he said that's possible. I said it is? He said, we are starting class just to train people to produce TV programs. I said you are? He said you can enroll. I said, I can? He said and it's free. I said it is? I was dumbfounded. I enrolled and went thru the complete training program.

APPOINTMENT WITH DEATH

Matthew 28.20, says. Christ speaking, Lo, I am with you always, even unto the end of the world. John 9.10 says, The thief cometh not, but for to steal, and to kill, and to destroy; I am come that they might have life, and that they might have it more abundantly. The Lord is faithful to His word.

My wife and I had been discussing, visiting our oldest daughter and her family for Christmas, for a couple of years. Since we usually travel in our 29 foot motor home, which has no respect for gas mileage, we had been putting the trip off. Around December 23rd, 1998, my wife and I, and our 13 year old grand-daughter headed for Birmingham, Alabama to spend Christmas with our daughter. The Lord had blessed us with enough money to make the trip. There was an ice storm moving toward Oklahoma City where we live, from the south that we didn't know about. We headed out of Oklahoma City, on I-40 East. When we reached the Oklahoma state line, we were in the ice storm, freezing rain was falling covering the highway, trees, power lines, everything. Our route carried us thru Arkansas, Tennessee, Mississippi, and then Alabama. There was ice all the way.

I have never seen so many cars and trucks jack-knifed and wrecked in all my life. Power lines were down everywhere, trees and power poles broken from the weight of the ice. Most of the traffic could only go 10 or 15 miles an hour and still they were sliding off the shoulder of the highway, or into the median, or into the west bound lanes of traffic, having wrecks. As I drove, I could feel the motor home lose traction as it slipped from one side of the lane I was traveling in, to the other. With the grace of God, we made it to our daughter's house. We spent Christmas Day with them and enjoyed the dinner that had been prepared. Sunday morning we went to our daughter's church for service. After service we embraced and said our good-bys, got on the highway and headed back to Oklahoma City.

As I write this portion of this book, I think about how well satan thought he and his plan was laid out to kill me and my family. Our motor home had two gas tanks. The main tank in the rear held 70 gallons of gas. The auxiliary tank which held 80 gallons was just behind the co-pilot's seat underneath. I had problems with this tank from day one of the purchase of the motor home. This was the first time I could not get gas to pump from this tank. I carried a full tank of gas to Alabama and started home with the same full tank. The weather had cleared and all the ice gone. We were wanting to get home after the long drive thru the ice there and the long ride back.

We had made it thru Mississippi, and was just outside of Memphis Tennessee, when I had a blow-out on the right side inside rear dual tire. I pulled over to the shoulder of the highway and jacked the motor home up and began to take the blown tire off and put my spare on. By the time I finished it was getting dark. I climbed back into the motor home and Evelyn said, Honey that wasn't bad. It only took you 45 minutes to change the tire. By the time we came thru Arkansas and had reached the Oklahoma state line, our grand-daughter, Angel had gone to sleep on the couch behind the driver's seat. Evelyn had reclined the co-pilot's seat and was dozing off and on. I had some gospel music playing and praising the Lord.

I passed a sign that said 49 or 50 miles to Oklahoma City. I checked the time and it was about 11:30 or 11:45, and I said Honey, we are almost home. All of a sudden two headlights appeared in front of me, right up on me. I said Honey here is a man on the wrong side of the highway. I'm driving the speed limit which is 70 miles an hour. I'm in the right lane of a divided highway and he is to. I tried to swerve to the left lane when there was a head-on collision. There was a loud crash and the sound of breaking glass and then silence. I was thrown into the ceiling still holding on the steering wheel. When I came down into the seat again, I looked over at my wife to see if she was alright. I didn't know it at the time, she was knocked unconscious and laying across the engine cover between the two front seats. Angel had been thrown to the floor and covered with all of our belongings that had been thrown from the cabinets and from the rear. All of this happened in seconds. Then I heard a sound as if someone had turned on a furnace and the flame has just come on. I looked to see where the sound was coming from and seen flames coming up into the motor home around the motor cover and my wife's face and arms.

I rushed to my wife's side while pulling her from the flames, telling her, honey this thing is on fire we have got to get out of here. She didn't respond. By that time Angel came to crying, Daddy what happened. I told her we had a head-on collision and to get out because the motor home was on fire. She ran to the door and tried to get out but came back hollering and crying saying the door is stuck and won't open. I set Evelyn in the floor still unconscious and went to the door. I kicked about three or four times before the door swung open. That front tank had ruptured and a flaming wall of gas was flowing past the door and Angel was afraid to go thru it. I grabbed her and shoved her thru the fire to safety. I returned and lifted Evelyn under both her arms and dragged her thru the fire and away from the burning motor home. Dying hadn't crossed my mind. The only thought in my mind was these gas tanks are going to explode and I've got to save my family. The driver of the other vehicle was killed on impact and then burned beyond recognition. People began to stop to see what had happened. It was cold and I had put my shoes on Evelyn's feet.

It took about 35 or 45 minutes before the Highway patrol or the emergency crew arrived. By that time the motor home was totally engulfed in flames. There was noting left but twisted metal. Our Christmas gifts, money, diamond rings, ministers license, ordination papers, keys to our house and keys to our cars, and all of our belongings. I go to the officer that arrives on the scene and gives him report of the accident. He says I know this was going to happen. We got a report that this guy had gotten on the wrong side of the highway 16 miles ahead of you. A mother and daughter driving a utility wagon had stopped and let Evelyn and Angel sit inside out of the cold. A helicopter arrives and carries Evelyn into Oklahoma City to the hospital. She has been complaining about pain in her side and how it was hard for her to breath. I wasn't hurt or feeling any pain other than the pain I suffer from four operations to my spine. One in my neck, one in my chest, and two in my lower back. Angel said she wasn't hurt. The two ladies who let Evelyn and Angel sit in their wagon, said they would bring Angel and myself into Oklahoma City. As soon as we got home, we changed clothes and notified our relatives of what had happened and went to the hospital where Evelyn was. She was in intensive care unit with two broken ribs, a broken collar bone, a punctured lung, and second and third degree burns to inside of her right arm from the wrist to her arm pit. While sitting with my wife, the attending nurse said that I needed to be checked to make sure I was alright. I told her I was fine. She insisted that I take x-rays and an MRI. I finally agreed. When the x-rays came back, the doctors came in where I was sitting with Evelyn, and told me that a vertebrae in my neck had punctured my spinal cord and that it was hemorrhaging and if I moved the wrong way I would be paralyzed from my neck down. I was rushed into surgery and came out with two vertebrae removed from my neck. A donor bone put in their place and a 2 inch long titanium plate with four screws holding things in place. We had many saints and friends and relatives to come and encourage us, as well as some pastors who came to our bed side. This portion of my book took place December 28, 1998. This is July 1999. Evelyn is completely healed, Angel is fine and I am still having pain in my neck and across my shoulders which I think is from the impact of the wreck while holding on to the steering wheel at 70 miles an hour. We are giving God all the praise and the glory for sparing our lives. He is precious in my soul and I love Him with all my heart.

THE SINS OF AMERICAN

There is sin and corruption from the white house to the church house. We have as a nation turned our backs on God. A little leaven, leavens the whole lump. In 1998, there were 2,233,000 marriages in America. At the same time there were, 1,135,000 divorces. The family is an institution of God. Divorces mean families torn apart. Exodus 32.6...says, and they rose up early on the morrow, and offered burnt offerings, and brought peace offerings; and the people sat down to eat and to drink, and rose up to play...after the people of this nation, go to church on Sunday, them that will even go, after service, the restaurants are packed.

The bars are open and beer and alcohol is consumed by the cases. The television is on across the nation and the sports has the peoples attention. After the people of Exodus. 32.6...had gotten drunk, the rising up to play suggests illicit and immoral sexual activity. In the years between 1992 and 1996 there were 4,258,210 abortions in this nation of, In God We Trust, in 1999, there was an estimated 88 million Americans 12 years older that had used illicit drugs at least once, 25 years and younger, and estimated 1,900,000 had used cocaine or crack and 10,000,000 had used marijuana at least once in the previous year.

In 1999, 51% of 12th graders used alcohol. In 1997, there were 32,166 fire arm deaths. From 1985 to 1999 there were 427,002 deaths from aids. For the same period of time, there were 687,863 new cases of aids. For the same period of time, there were men with men transmitted aids, 330,193 cases.

In 1999, there were, out of a population of 272,691,000, 15,530 murder or manslaughter cases. There were 89,000 forcible rapes, 409,670 robberies. In 1999 there were 1,305,393 people sentenced to prison for more than a year. According to justice department figures and estimates, as of 2000, there are 2,000,000 people behind bars, and 4,500,000 more people are on probation and parole.

Jeremiah 5.1 thru 5...Run ye to and fro through the streets of Jerusalem, and see now, and know, and seek in the broad places thereof, if ye can find a man, if there be any that executeth judgment, that seeketh the truth; and I will pardon it. And though they say, the Lord liveth; surely they swear falsely...O Lord, are not thine eyes upon the truth? Thou hast stricken them, but they have not grieved; Thou has consumed them, but they have refused to receive correction; they have made their faces harder than a rock, they have refused to return...therefore I said, surely these are poor; they are foolish; for they know not the way of the Lord, nor the judgment of their God...I will get me unto the great men, and will speak unto them; for they have known the way of the Lord, and the judgment of their God; but these have altogether broken the yoke, and burst the bonds.

Jeremiah 5.7 thru 12...Jeremiah was speaking to a nation that had turned their back on God just as this nation has. Because of the corruption and sin and the 4,258,210 abortions in this nation, the land runs red with the blood of the innocent babies...The Lord God in Jeremiah speaks and says...How shall I pardon thee for this? Thy children have forsaken me, and sworn by them that are no Gods; when I had fed them to the full, they then committed adultery, and assembled themselves by troops in the harlots houses...they were as fed horses in the morning; everyone neighed after his neighbors wife.

Jeremiah 5.9 thru 12...The word of God to Jeremiah for the nation of Israel and to America, ...shall I not visit for these things? Saith the Lord; and shall not my soul be avenged on such a nation as this? ...go ye upon her walls, and destroy; but make not a full end; take away her battlements; for they are not the Lord's...for the house of Israel and the house of Judah have dealt very treacherously against me, saith the Lord...they have belied the Lord, and said it is not he; neither shall evil come upon us; neither shall we see sword nor famine. 15...Lo, I will bring a nation upon you from far, O house of Israel, saith the Lord; it is a mighty nation, it is a ancient nation, a nation whose language thou knowest not, neither understandest what they say.

Jeremiah 7.5 thru 10...For if you thoroughly amend your ways and your doings; if you thoroughly execute judgment between a man and his neighbor; ...if you oppress not the stranger, the fatherless, and the widow, and shed not innocent blood in this place, neither walk after other gods to your hurt; ...then will I cause you to dwell in this place, in the land that I gave to your fathers, for ever and ever...Behold, ye trust in lying words, that cannot profit...will you steal, murder, and commit adultery, and swear falsely, and burn incense unto Baal, and walk after gods whom ye know not; and come and stand before me in this house, and say, we are delivered to do all these abominations? Verses 11 & 12, is this house, which is called by my name, become a den of robbers in your eyes? Behold, even I have seen it, saith the Lord...but go ye now unto the place which was in Shilo, where I set my name at the first, and see what I did to it for the wickedness of my people Israel.

Jeremiah 23.20 thru 24...The anger of the Lord shall not return, until He have executed, and until He have performed the thoughts of His heart; in the latter days ye shall consider it perfectly...I have not sent these prophets, yet they ran; I have not spoken to them, yet they prophesied...but if they had stood in my counsel, and had caused my people to hear my words, then they should have turned them from their evil way, and from the evil of their doings...am I a God at hand, saith the Lord, and not a God afar off? ...can any hide himself in secret places that I shall not see him? saith the Lord. Do not I fill heaven and earth? saith the Lord.

Job 19.29...Be ye afraid of the sword, for wrath bringeth the punishments of the sword, that ye may know there is a judgment.

Psalm 1.5...Therefore the ungodly shall not stand in the judgment, nor sinners in the congregation of the righteous.

Psalm 25.9...The meek shall He guide in judgment; and the meek will He teach the way.

Isaiah 26.9...With my soul have I desired thee in the night, yea with my spirit within me will I seek thee early, for when thy judgments are in the earth, inhabitants of the world will learn righteousness.

Isaiah 1.27 & 27...Zion shall be redeemed with judgment, and her converts with righteousness...and the destruction of the transgressors and of the sinners shall be together, and they that forsake the Lord shall be consumed.

I John 4.16 & 17...And we have known and believed the love that God hath to us. God is love; and he that dwelleth in love dwelleth in God, and God in him...Herein is our love made perfect, that we may have boldness in the day of judgment; because as he is, so are we in this world.

May the anointing that is upon this book, cause you to seek Him while He may be found. I truly hope that something I have said, will draw you to the Lord before it is to late.

<u>May God Bless You</u>

<u>The Watchman On The Wall</u>

Lifting up my voice like a trumpet to warn of

<u>The</u>

<u>Judgments of America</u>

Written by:..Elder E.L. Staley

THE WATCHMAN ON THE WALL

LIFTING UP MY VOICE LIKE A TRUMPET TO WARN OF THE JUDGMENTS OF AMERICA

ABOUT THE AUTHOR

I am a sixty-two-year old black ordained Elder in the Church of God in Christ. The book tells of the suffering I had to endure as a child and into adulthood and the call of God to be a voice in the wilderness to this nation of the coming judgments that God is about to bring upon this nation.

I've been in at least six situations where I knew I was going to die, but God brought me out, and many of those times without a scratch. I have been with the woman I know God sent to me for thirty-four years. Evelyn, my wife, has been faithful to me from day one, and has willingly supported me most of our marriage because of my disability resulting from many surgeries to the spine.

www.ingramcontent.com/pod-product-compliance
Ingram Content Group UK Ltd.
Pitfield, Milton Keynes, MK11 3LW, UK
UKHW040016200726
13854UKWH00001B/236